Collector's Guide to

Willow Ware

Jennifer A. Lindbeck

Schiffer Publishing Ltd

4880 Lower Valley Road, Atglen, PA 19310 USA

Library of Congress Cataloging-in-Publication Data

Lindbeck, Jennifer A.
A collector's guide to willow ware /Jennifer A. Lindbeck.
p. cm.
Includes bibliographical references and index.
ISBN: 0-7643-1055-0 (pbk.)
1. Willow ware--Collectors and collecting--Catalogs. I. Title: Book of willow ware. II. Title.
NK4277.L56 2000
738.3'7--dc21
99-057142

Designed by Bonnie M. Hensley
Type set in BernhardMod BT/Times New Roman

ISBN: 0-7643-1055-0
Printed in China
1 2 3 4

Published by Schiffer Publishing Ltd. 4880 Lower Valley Road Atglen, PA 19310 Phone: (610) 593-1777; Fax: (610) 593-2002 E-mail: Schifferbk@aol.com Please visit our web site catalog at **www.schifferbooks.com**	In Europe, Schiffer books are distributed by Bushwood Books 6 Marksbury Avenue Kew Gardens Surrey TW9 4JF England Phone: 44 (0)208-392-8585; Fax: 44 (0)208-392-9876 E-mail: Bushwd@aol.com Free postage in UK. Europe: air mail at cost.

This book may be purchased from the publisher.
Include $3.95 for shipping. Please try your bookstore first.
We are interested in hearing from authors with book ideas on related subjects.
You may write for a free printed catalog.

Dedication

To my parents, Ron and Sue Lindbeck, who have made so many
of my accomplishments memorable and worthwhile.

Acknowledgments

There are many people whose assistance, knowledge, and experience were extremely valuable and instrumental in helping to bring this project to fruition: to collectors Tim & Kim Allen and Bill & Joyce Keenan, I extend my warmest gratitude for their willingness to open their homes and collections to me and my colleague, Donna Baker—their expertise and enthusiasm for the subject proved indispensible; to collectors Pat & Ken Roberts, Dennis Crosby, Tom & Barbara Allen, Louise M. Loehr of Louise's Old Things, Michael L. Curtner, Keith A. Brower, Shirely & Jim Hillier, and Jeanne Berlew, who were kind enough to allow me to photograph a few choice pieces from their collections—meeting with each was my pleasure; to the members of the International Willow Collectors (IWC) for their friendliness, and passion for the subject of willow; to Donna Baker, whose experience, teaching, and numerous contributions to this project were greatly valued and highly regarded; to Doug Congdon-Martin and Peter Schiffer, whose patience and confidence did not go unnoticed nor unappreciated; to my friends and family, for their moral support and encouragement—each of you bring such joy to my life; and to the rest of the designers and staff at Schiffer Publishing whose hard work and effort make my job here enjoyable and satisfying.

Contents

Preface

A quick glance at the Contents page will afford you a good idea of this book's organization. Items are grouped according to shape (e.g., plates, platters, pitchers); function or use (e.g., coffee & tea, condiment pieces, items for bed & bath); and type of material (e.g., paper products, fabrics). To best show off the willow pattern and introduce you to its array of patterns and variations, I have placed the chapter on plates at the beginning. Plates display a wide surface area, on an open plane; they feature an overall visual image of a pattern, allowing you to view the pattern in its entirety (and without interruption, such as might occur on a rounded or more shapely vessel). More often than not, the manufacturer's mark is also made quite visible on a plate, making identification easier, and at times even permissible. Studying the chapter on plates (and the plates that you have in your collection) will acquaint you with the various patterns and enable you to recognize and distinguish between them; you can then start to make connections with other items. You may discover that the pattern of an unmarked ware matches a plate that you've been able to identify. These connections come with time, experience, and familiarity with the subject matter; they build a novice collector/collection into one that is more solid and learned.

For quick and easy access to information on items, caption information is presented in a specific order—item name, measurements (in the order of height, length, width, depth, and diameter, unless otherwise noted), type of material (if earthenware, this is assumed), description of pattern and/or any specific information concerning an item, manufacturer (if unlisted, this information is unknown), place of origin (including town/city and country, when known), whether the piece is marked or impressed on the bottom (if unlisted, the item is unmarked or contains a mark corresponding to its place of manufacture), and approximate date of manufacture. For the sake of consistency and accuracy in the identification of items, I have used Geoffrey Godden's *Encyclopaedia of British Pottery and Porcelain Marks* whenever possible, referencing Arnold and Dorothy Kowalsky's *Encyclopedia of Marks 1780-1980*, Ralph & Terry Kovel's *Kovel's New Dictionary of Marks*, and Lois Lehner's *Lehner's Encyclopedia of U.S. Marks on Pottery, Porcelain, & Clay,* when the information was unavailable in Godden's. In some instances, I have included mark numbers from these sources for the purposes of cross-referencing.

In this book, the terms polychrome and multicolor(ed) are used interchangeably. However,

in some present-day willow circles, polychrome pertains to multicolored willow of English manufacture, while the term multicolor is reserved for American items. Differentiation need also be made between Gaudy Willow and clobbered. Technically speaking, all Gaudy Willow is clobbered, or over painted with multicolor embellishments, but not all clobbered willow is Gaudy. (The name Gaudy Willow was first used by Buffalo Pottery Co., of Buffalo, New York, to refer to their clobbered wares.) For the purposes of this book, Gaudy Willow is used only to refer to clobbered items manufactured by Buffalo Pottery Co. More generally, Gaudy has been adopted as the American term for clobbered willow, and sometimes may be applied to clobbered wares of English manufacture—Ridgways and Wedgwood are two examples.

Additional information on pattern variations, manufacturers' marks (including detailed photographs of pattern variations and marks, when possible), manufacturers, town/country of origin, and aspects of historical background may be expanded upon in the captions or text to provide further insight to readers. Because manufacturers were not always consistent in the marking of wares (as you may have discovered already), and backstamps, manufacturers' names, location of factories, etc. changed in such dizzying array, it is virtually impossible to avoid all chance of error in the identification of items. With so many factors fluctuating, complete identification of an item is not always possible.

Prices in the captions are presented in a range, and, as with any price guide, these values are not meant to set firm prices. They are meant, however, to give collectors and dealers a relative idea of the range in price expected for a particular item and to point out items that are particularly rare or valuable. In determining an item's value, it is important to consider all factors: availability, condition, age, collectibility, rarity, desirability, and geographical location. The prices compiled herein are not the result of the author's nor the collectors' calculations, but have been provided by an outside source. Neither the author nor the publisher are responsible for any outcomes resulting from using this guide.

I hope that this book and the photographs and information herein may serve to enrich your knowledge and love of willow ware in its many variations of color, pattern, shape, and border design.

Introduction to Willow

When first approached to be the next author of a book on willow ware, I was both excited and overwhelmed by the challenge—it seemed to me quite an undertaking. Previous to my research, I knew of the willow pattern through my mother and grandmother. It was the pattern that adorned the everyday plates in my mother's kitchen and the dishes of grandmother. Yet never at the time did I imagine the vastness of the willow pattern, the diversity of color, shape, and variant pattern, and variety of items willow encompasses.

I began my research of willow ware on the Internet, which holds a wealth of knowledge and may be a good place for you to start in your quest for willow and information on the subject. I discovered the web page for the International Willow Collectors society (IWC), and was able to contact Tim Allen, IWC member, co-chair of the IWC 1999 convention, and owner of many fine willow ware items; over the course of 1999, I had the great pleasure of photographing and "seeing" his extensive collection, along with various other collections. It was through the viewing and photographing of these pieces of willow, and my further research on the subject, that I came soon to realize that collecting willow means much more than the traditional blue and white patterned plates of my grandma's and mother's kitchen.

The intricacies of the willow pattern are vast: it appears in many assorted colors, apart from the traditionally-thought-of blue and white (see for yourself the yellow, brown, pink, pale blue, green, black, and even lavender wares that bear the willow pattern); with many variations on the traditional willow design; in variant patterns; with multicolor and hand painted embellishments; and with a multiplicity of traditional and unusual border designs.

History

Traditions for blue and white patterned designs like that of the willow pattern lie rooted in chinoiserie—designs on printed ceramics derived from the Oriental style of decoration—and in the Chinese porcelain wares imported to England during the sixteenth, seventeenth, and eighteenth centuries. During the latter part of the eighteenth century, English manufacturers developed their own means to produce wares decorated in the Oriental style of decoration: the willow pattern arose as a direct competitor with imported Chinese decorated wares, and soon became a favorite. Sources differ on the exact date of development for the willow pattern and by whom, making complete knowlege of the pattern's origin and development somewhat uncertain. Some claim the well-known **Josiah S. Spode** as the pattern's originator, copying the pattern from one known as the Two Birds Chinese pattern and calling it Mandarin; he is credited with the conception of the willow pattern around 1790, and as the first producer of the pattern known today as the traditional around 1810. Other sources ascribe the pattern's beginnings to **Thomas Turner** or **Thomas Minton** at Caughley, a pottery located in Shropshire, England, (est. 1750 to 1814), around the 1780s. The **Wedgwood firm** is also named as contributing to the pattern's development, adopting a version of the willow pattern in the 1790s.

Some sources draw parallels and connecting lines between several or a few designers and dates—designed by Thomas Minton, an engraver who worked at Caughley, which was owned by Thomas Turner; introduced by Thomas Turner at Caughley in 1780, and then copied and altered by Thomas Minton; and so on. Because the web of dates and designers for the willow pattern has grown to be even more elaborate and diversified over the centuries of its production, precise attribution of the pattern to one individual on a specific date has become all the more obscure—for in fact, since its beginning, many designers, manufacturers, and others have contributed toward the pattern's proliferation and success!

Despite any inconsistancies in past accounts of the pattern's history, most sources agree to the late eighteenth century as the time period when the pattern was first introduced, with it being refined and adapted into the traditional willow pattern, as it is known today, by 1810. The pattern's infectious popularity, most immediately following its development, however, is indisputable: by 1830, nearly 200 makers of the willow pattern existed (Hughes 158), a number which later would come to reflect the number of potteries in England *alone* manufacturing willow-patterned wares (Quintner 210). From the pattern's development in the late 1700s and on to the present day, countless numbers of manufacturers have replicated and reproduced the pattern (Godden, 1969), with nearly all of the Staffordshire potters at one time or another using the pattern or variations of it in the decoration of wares (Camehl 288). It has endured and outlasted through many aesthetic art movements—Gothic Revival, Romanticism, Federal, Victorianism, Arts & Crafts, Art Nouveau, Art Deco—(Quintner 147); earned rightful recognition as a time-honored classic and one of the most distinguishable and cherished patterns in ceramics; and, of course, established its universal appeal among willow enthusiasts, ceramic collectors, and dealers alike.

The Willow Legend

"So she tells me a legend centuries old
Of a Mandarin rich in lands and gold,
Of Koon-Shee fair and Chang the good,
Who loved each other as lovers should.
How they hid in the gardener's hut awhile,
Then fled away to the beautiful isle.
Though a cruel father pursued them there,
And would have killed the hopeless pair,
But kindly power, by pity stirred,
Changed each into a beautiful bird.

Here is the orange tree where they talked,
Here they are running away,
And over all at the top you see
The bird making love alway."
[*The Blue-China Book*, by Ada Walker Camehl, 287]

Development of the willow pattern and its popularity are due in part to the legend behind the pattern—centuries old, the legend has changed and been modified with the passing of time. The individual elements that compose the willow pattern are each representative of an aspect of the legend and the events that take place therein.

There are nearly as many versions of the willow legend as there are variations on the pattern and manufacturers that reproduce it. Though it varies widely, the basic story line can be summarized as follows: a wealthy Mandarin, Li-Chi, who lived in a lavish temple or pagoda-like home surrounded by willow trees and other beautiful and rare vegetation, forced his male secretary, Chang, who is supposed to live in the smaller house across the water, into some backhanded dealings. After the wealthy merchant's wife dies suddenly, he decides to dismiss his secretary. However, Chang meanwhile has fallen deeply in love with the man's daughter, Koong-Shee; once word of the affair reaches the father, he forbids it, and betroths his daughter, instead, to a wealthy Duke, Ta-jin. Though forbidden to see each other, Chang and Koong-Shee continue their love for one another, relaying love

letters back and forth by boat. On the night that Koong-Shee is to be wed to the Duke, Chang rescues her and together they travel to a sequestered island to live. Years later, Ta-jin, the Duke, discovers Koong-Shee's whereabouts, and the location of the island. He travels to the island to fight to reclaim her love. During the battle, Chang loses his life, and, out of love for him, Koong-Shee takes her own.

Over the centuries that the pattern has been in existence, many have speculated on the symbolism and relevance of the various elements that comprise the pattern. Knowing the basic premise behind the design provides some insight into the different possible interpretations of its elements. For example, the birds in the pattern may be an allusion to the spirits of the two lovers (Maust 12, 23), while the figures on the bridge may represent Koong-Shee (figure holding staff), Chang (figure with box of jewels), and Li-Chi (figure with whip) (Coysh 403). Variations in the depiction of these pattern elements and others do occur widely. Noticing these alterations may offer you a different perspective on the legend, or even lead you to develop a new-fashioned version of the legend on your own.

The Willow Pattern and the Transfer-Printing Process

Though appealing due to its legendary beginnings, we owe much of the perfusion of the willow pattern and its widespread use to the process of transfer printing and the impact its development had on the production and manufacture of decorated wares.

The transfer-printing process was first developed for use on china in 1751 by an Irish-born engraver named John Brooks (Brooke 1). Several individuals were involved in the process, including the engraver, cutter, transferor, and apprentice. First, an outline of the design would be traced by the engraver from paper onto a piece of tissue paper; the design was then transferred to a copper sheet using homemade carbon paper. Details and shading in the form of grooves, lines, and/or dots were added to the copper sheet design. Largely, the quality of the transfer print depended upon the quality of the copper engraving: the deeper the engraving, the darker the color and richer the details and shading. (Also, the quality was dependent upon the type of method used to add details and shading: lines are more common in designs predating 1800, while dots or stippling, a more refined technique, were used in post-1800 patterns.)

The ink coloring for the design was kept warm on a circular iron plate (or backstone). At first, cobalt blue was the only avaliable color used in the decoration of wares, most likely chosen because it could withstand the heat of the kilns and remain intact. (Later, however, around the 1830s, methods were refined for the use of a variety of colors underglaze.) The ink stain was applied to the copper sheet and carefully made to fill all the crevices of the design; any excess was scraped and rubbed off, so that the sheet was clean.

Tissue paper coated with a soap and water mixture was used to transfer the pattern of the design from the copper sheet to the ware. The tissue paper was placed on the copper sheet, and the design imprinted onto the tissue paper by passing the copper sheet with applied tissue paper through the press's rollers. (The image of the design now appeared in reverse on the tissue paper. Over time, improvements were made in the quality of the tissue paper used, which allowed for improvements in the quality of the transfer-print and for finer patterns in the design.) Next, the tissue was removed from the copper sheet and sent to the cutter. He would remove any excess tissue paper, leaving only the design. Next, the transferor placed the design on the ware, which had already been fired for the first time in the kiln, and used a stiff bristle brush to secure the design to the ware. (It was at this time that the transferor was responsible for the application of the manufacturer's mark to the bottom or back of the ware; sometimes, this was overlooked, whether intentionally or otherwise, thus resulting in unmarked wares.)

After the design was applied, the ware was dipped into the glaze, refired, and once out of the kiln, soaked in water by the apprentice to soften the paper for removal. (The printed design remained intact on the ware because the coloring was of an oil-base.) If a ware were to have both a center and border design, the center pattern would be applied first and then the border. Once dry, the ware was fired again in the hardening kiln, which also removed any excess oil and set the color. The ware was then glazed for a second time and refired for the last time. It was during this glaze firing that some flowing might occur in the coloring of the pattern. Later, this flowed or flown effect was encouraged through the addition of a chemical to the glaze, resulting in what has popularly come to be known as flow(n) blue wares.

An example of a piece of willow ware in which the pattern was flown or flowed. Oval platter, 12.875" x 10.25", flow blue, by Doulton & Co., Burslem, England, c. 1930+. *Courtesy of Joyce & Bill Keenan.*

Mark of platter.

Reverse of flow blue platter, showing "bleeding" or blurring in the color of the pattern onto back.

Transfer printing changed the face of decorated wares, allowing for the same design or pattern to be reproduced over and over on a variety of wares. Less expensive than hand painting, more precise, more expeditious, and requiring fewer number of skilled artisans, it made mass production and the production of sets of wares printed with the same, identical pattern possible.

However, because patterns were applied to the wares by hand, using the pieces of tissue paper, it could not be ensured that pattern designs would match up completely. You may notice mismatched lines in a pattern, indicating that pieces of the tissue paper were mislaid or not matched up exactly by the transferor. The term "incomplete" or "uneven" transfer (print) is used to refer to imperfections such as this. As well, incomplete transfers were required for the more curved or shapely objects, or smaller ones such as butter pats and curved objects such as teapots often required some pattern parts to be cut away. Looking at the details of the transfer print can afford you insight into the make and quality (even date and origin) of your pieces—noticing these minute details will allow you to view your pieces (or those you may acquire) with a sense of uniqueness and sensitivity to their individual character.

With regard to the willow pattern, transfer printing was first used during the early 1800s in the decoration of pearlware. (For more information on pearlware, see Chapter One: Plates, page 42.) With the development of transfer printing, the willow pattern (and others) could be more easily duplicated and freely copied by other factories, thus allowing for its widespread use among many factories throughout England. Eventually countries other than England also developed the means to produce wares using the methods of transfer printing—the process spread throughout Europe, with manufacturers in Germany, Holland, France, and Austria, to name a few, producing wares decorated in the willow pattern. It was not until the turn from the nineteenth to the twentieth century, however, that the technique was refined for use by American manufacturers in the decoration of willow-patterned wares. (For more information on willow produced in other countries, see page 30; for willow manufactured in America, see Chapter One, page 54.) Future refinement and adjustment to the ink used and the techinque itself eventually allowed for the production of wares in a variety of colors. Later, methods such as decalcomania, a form of transfer printing, and rubber-stamping emerged, which further contributed toward the mass production of wares decorated in the willow pattern and permitted its production in a variety of colors. (Snyder, 1995, 16-20; Hughes, 1968, 148, 150-152; Brooke, 1999, 1, 14; Worth, 1991, 8-10; Snyder, 1992, 15-16; Snyder, 1994, 4-7)

Pattern Variations

Since the willow pattern's introduction in the late eighteenth to early nineteenth centuries, the pattern has been widely replicated and reproduced (this due in part to the development of the

While border patterns almost always had to be cut to fit, these two border details exhibit similar characteristics to uneven or incomplete transfer prints.

Detail showing **Traditional pattern** as featured on circa 1810 plate. As defined by Robert Copeland of Spode, the traditional pattern consists of a "bridge with three persons crossing it, the willow tree, the boat, the main tea house, the two birds, and a fence across foreground of the garden." Also included is a figure in the boat (a total of four figures in all), an orange tree, fir tree, and possibly other Oriental-looking types of vegetation.

transfer-printing process, which was previously noted). As a result, many slight variations and interpretations of the pattern exist. In some cases, manufacturers would alter the pattern slightly, devising their own interpretations of the overall design and/or various pattern elements. Some manufacturers became known for their use of a particular verision of the pattern—distinguishing their willow wares through depiction or alteration of the traditional pattern elements, or exclusion of particular elements in prominent display of others. The more common of these variations on the willow pattern are identified by name. Sometimes there is a direct correlation between the pattern name and the name of the manufacturer that produced/introduced the version of the pattern. Each variation is distinguishable by its particular depiction of the pattern and pattern elements. Close examination of your willow will allow you to notice slight variations in the pattern and pattern elements. Recognizing the various patterns and learning to distinguish between them may provide for some excit-

ing new discoveries in the world of willow. (The descriptions of the patterns herein are complied largely from Mary Frank Gaston's *Blue Willow: An Identification and Value Guide*, a handout entitled "Willow Pattern China: A brief study of the Willow pattern: Its variations and history," and author's own observations.)

Detail showing **Mandarin pattern** in red. Considered to be the original willow pattern engraved by Thomas Minton for Thomas Turner at the Caughley factory, circa 1790, and the pattern that most closely resembles the traditional pattern. (However, sources do differ in their attribution of this pattern to a single individual.) It is distinguished by the appearance of one figure in the boat, which appears under the willow tree, the dagger (or fleur-de-lis) border, and the absence of the bridge, fence, and additional figures seen in other versions of the willow pattern.

Detail of **Burleigh pattern**. Considered one of two willow variant patterns true to the traditional pattern; the English manufacturer Burgess & Leigh Co., from which the name originates, produced the majority of wares decorated in this pattern. The pattern was first produced in 1920s, but was not in full production until 1929. It can be distinguished by the appearance of five figures, the scroll and flower border, and lacking the element of the orange tree.

Detail of **Booths pattern**. This pattern contains all the elements of the traditional pattern, but lacks the appearance of the fence in the foreground and the second pagoda or temple on the island (seen in traditional pattern at bottom left). The element of the willow tree is depicted with six branches on the left and three on right; the bow knot design is characteristic of the border. Though imitated by Japanese manufacturers, such as NKT (or Nihon Koshitsu Toki Company) or Nikko Porcelain, the Booths pattern was developed by Booths pottery of Tunstall, England, and, by 1912, had taken on the look it has today.

Detail showing plate decorated in imitation of Booths pattern, but made by NKT (or Nihon Koshitsu Toki Company) and marked Double Phoenix (shown in pink). The Double Phoenix mark often appears on pieces of willow ware that are of Japanese manufacturer and decorated in imitation of the Booths pattern.

Detail of **Two Temples I pattern**. Referred to as "Pagoda" by Caughley and "Two Temples" by Spode, this pattern was introduced circa 1810, but based on original hand painted designs from about 1780. Its name, coined by Robert Copeland in *Spode's Willow Pattern & Other Designs after the Chinese*, refers to the two overlapping temples on left (later discovered to be just one temple with an inside courtyard giving the illusion of a second temple). The placement of willow tree below the bridge helps to distinguish the pattern from Two Temples II. Other distinguishing elements are the four figures (two on arch bridge, one in the temple doorway, and one on the rocks) and often times the appearance of the butterfly border design. The pattern is considered quite rare and only to be found on older willow pieces.

Detail showing **Two Temples II pattern**. Introduced in 1817, this pattern closely resembles the Two Temples I pattern with the exception of the placement of the willow tree and the fourth figure that appears on the rocks. This pattern was much more commonly used than the Two Temples I pattern and particular elements of the pattern varied from manufacturer to manufacturer according to their adaptation of it. One adaptation of the pattern shows it reversed, with the temple on the right, and is referred to as Two Temples II reversed.

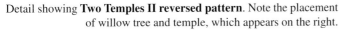

Detail showing **Two Temples II reversed pattern**. Note the placement of willow tree and temple, which appears on the right.

Detail of **Turner pattern**. Named for the English potter John Turner, this design was originated between the years 1810-1812 and can be distinguished by the appearance of two figures on the bridge, the scroll and flower border pattern, and the absence of the birds, boats, and fence.

Two details showing variation in depiction of birds. Pattern at top shows birds with split tails. Willow produced by Japanese manufacturers tended to depict birds of a "plumper" variety. Look closely at your willow ware for slight variations in pattern and elements within the pattern. Recognizing variations in pattern and pattern elements may unearth some exciting new discoveries in the world of willow.

Detail showing **Worcester pattern** in brown. Used by Worcester Royal Porcelain Company, of Worcester, England (hence the name), this pattern can be distinguished by the appearance of three figures, three boats, a pagoda or temple with fence on either side of the water, the scroll and flower border (though example shows the dagger or fluer-de-lis border), a bridge at upper left, and several variations of trees. The elements of the orange and willow tree and birds, however, are altogether absent from the pattern. The classification of the Worcester pattern as a part of the willow family is much disputed as the pattern bears little resemblance to the traditional willow pattern. Despite the controversy, many willow ware collectors enjoy this pattern and are quite happy to add a piece to their willow collection.

Border Patterns

In addition to the many variations and adaptations of the willow pattern, willow ware can also be found with an array of traditional and unusual border designs, simple line borders, or the absence of a border design altogether. Some border patterns may have names that are familiar to you, while others may be unique to a specific manufacturer or have yet to be documented. Of particular interest are pieces with polychrome or hand painted border designs, as well as pieces that feature traditional border elements in a new arrangement or in combination with an unusual center pattern. Be on the lookout for these items (in your travels and in the pages that follow).

Detail showing example of tradition willow border pattern.

Detail showing another example of traditional willow border.

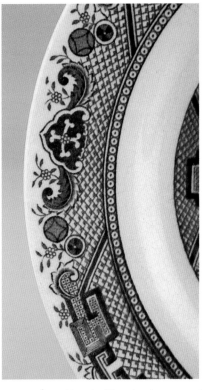

Detail of traditional willow border reversed.

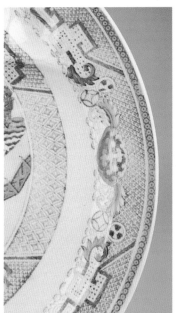

Detail of traditional willow border with hand painting overglaze, also known as clobbering.

Detail of fish-roe—a common element shown in border design and/or as embellishment elsewhere on piece.

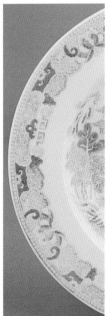

Detail of butterfly border in pale blue.

Detail of butterfly border in multicolor.

Detail showing bow knot border.

Detail of variation of scroll and flower border with hand painted embellishment both over and under the glaze.

Detail showing dagger or fluer-de-lis border design, commonly seen in combination with Mandarin pattern.

Three details showing slight variations in scroll and flower border.

Black

Dinner plate, 10" dia., with scalloped edge,
pearlware, black traditional pattern, England,
c. 1810. *Courtesy of Tim & Kim Allen.* $75-125.

Mulberry

Plate, 12 sided, 9" dia., mulberry
willow, England, c. 1850. *Courtesy
of Tim & Kim Allen.* $75-100.

Pink

Plate, 8" dia., pink willow, by William Adams & Sons Ltd., Tunstall and Stoke, England, c. 1893-1917. *Courtesy of Joyce & Bill Keenan.* $35-50.

Sugar bowl, no lid, 2.5" h., pink willow, by Homer Laughlin China Co., East Liverpool, Ohio, USA, c. 1938+. *Courtesy of Joyce & Bill Keenan.* $10-15; with lid: $25-30.

Teapot, 4.5" h., pink willow, by Homer Laughlin China Co., East Liverpool, Ohio, USA, c. 1938+. *Courtesy of Tim & Kim Allen.* $75-100.

Large creamer, 4" h., and sugar with lid, 5" h., pink willow, Japan.
Courtesy of Joyce & Bill Keenan. $15 each; $60-75 for set.

Grill plate, 9.5" dia., pink willow, by Walker China Co., Bedford, Ohio, USA, c. 1947. *Courtesy of Joyce & Bill Keenan.* $25-35.

Mark of plate.

Plate, 10" dia., pink willow, Japanese version of Booths pattern with bow knot border, by NKT (or Nihon Koshitsu Toki Company), Japan. *Courtesy of Tim & Kim Allen.* $40-50.

Brown

Creamer, 6" h., brown willow, England. *Courtesy of Joyce & Bill Keenan.* $95-125.

Grill plate, 9" dia., brown willow, by Sterling China Co., East Liverpool, Ohio, USA. *Courtesy of Joyce & Bill Keenan.* $25-35.

Oval platter, 8.75" x 11.625", brown willow, Worcester pattern, by Worcester Royal Porcelain Company Ltd., Worcester, England, c. 1885. *Courtesy of Joyce & Bill Keenan.* $125-165.

Coffee pot, 8.5 h., brown willow, unmarked though attributed to Crown Staffordshire Porcelain Co. Ltd., Fenton, England, c. 1906+. *Courtesy of Michael L. Curtner.* $250-300.

Alternate view of coffee pot showing decorative ribbon and bow near handle and on top of lid.

Green

Grill plate, 10.375" dia., green willow, England, marked "Made in England/ Registered Design/#712950/6/33," c. 1933. *Courtesy of Joyce & Bill Keenan.* $35-45.

Ginger jar with lid, 4.5" h., 4.25" dia., green willow, by G.L. Ashworth & Bros., Fenton, England, c. 1891+. *Courtesy of Joyce & Bill Keenan.* $75-100.

Lavender

Platter, 9.75" x 12.25", lilac or lavender willow, Kang-he pattern, by Thomas Till & Sons, Burslem, England, c. 1922-8. Note the manufacturer's pattern name that appears in the mark. *Courtesy of Jeanne Berlew.* $150-175.

Mark of platter.

Red

Mark of plate.

Plate, 10.25" dia., with scalloped edge, red willow, mandarin pattern, by W. T. Copeland, Stoke, England, c. 1937. Note the appearance of the manufacturer's pattern name above the mark. *Courtesy of Joyce & Bill Keenan.* $45-60.

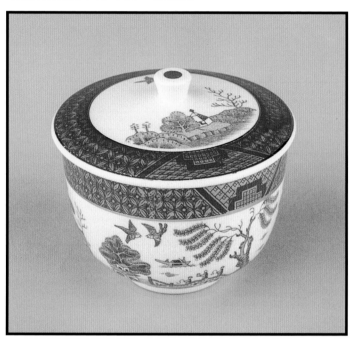

Teacup with lid, 2.25" h., 3.25" dia., red willow, Japanese version of Booths pattern with bow knot border, by NKT (or Nihon Koshitsu Toki Company), Japan, marked "Double Phoenix" by manufacturer. *Courtesy of Joyce & Bill Keenan.* $60-75.

Oval platter, 5.875" x 8.25", red willow, by Buffalo China Co., Buffalo, New York, USA, c. 1915+. *Courtesy of Joyce & Bill Keenan.* $60-75.

Pale Blue

Octagonal-shaped covered vegetable dish with lid, 9" x 8.5", pale blue, Two Temples II pattern with butterfly border, by W. T. Copeland, Stoke, England, March 1883. *Courtesy of Joyce & Bill Keenan.* $225-260.

Teapot, 6.5" h., pale blue, Two Temples II reversed pattern with butterfly border, England, c. mid-1800s. *Courtesy of Joyce & Bill Keenan.* $325-375.

Soup bowl, 9.25" dia., pale blue, Two Temples II pattern, by W. T. Copeland, Stoke, England, March 1883. *Courtesy of Joyce & Bill Keenan.* $50-60.

Rice bowl (or waste bowl), 2.875" h., 5.5" dia., pale blue, Two Temples II pattern with butterfly border on inside of bowl, by W. T. Copeland, Stoke, England, March 1883. *Courtesy of Joyce & Bill Keenan.* $125-175 (waste bowl is more valuable).

Alternate view showing interior of bowl.

Teacup and saucer, pale blue, Two Temples II pattern with butterfly border, unmarked though attributed to W. T. Copeland, Stoke, England. *Courtesy of Joyce & Bill Keenan.* $75-125 mint; $50-75 as is. (Tea can cause discoloration to items depreciating the value.)

Gravy pitcher (or server), 4" h., pale blue, Two Temples II pattern, England. *Courtesy of Joyce & Bill Keenan.* $100-150.

Willow from around the World

In addition to the countless number of manufacturers in England, America, and Japan that utilized the willow pattern in the decoration of tableware and other items, the pattern and many variations have been employed by manufacturers in countries around the world. The following photographs present a modest selection of willow ware items produced in countries other than England, America, or Japan. In your travels (around the world or simply around the country), you may want to fetch a piece of willow as a souvenir to remind you of the towns you have visited or to mark some of the places you travelled to on your journey—create your own personalized collection of willow from around the world.

Teapot, 6.5" h. (to top of finial), enamel, dark blue with willow pattern on sides, Austria. *Courtesy of Joyce & Bill Keenan.* $225-275.

Tin, 4.75" h., Australia. *Courtesy of Tim & Kim Allen.* $85-125.

Mark of plate.

Plate, 9.75" dia., porcelain, multicolor variant pattern with pictorial border, marked "Victoria/ Czecho-slovakia." *Courtesy of Tim & Kim Allen.* $75-100.

Mark of platter.

Oval platter, 8.75" x 12.625", by Grands Establissements Ceramique Nord, France, c. pre-1891. *Courtesy of Joyce & Bill Keenan.* $75-100.

Mark of grill plate.

Grill plate, 10.25" dia., by Villeroy & Boch, Wallerfangen, Germany, 1876-1931. *Courtesy of Joyce & Bill Keenan.* $40-50.

WILLOW
MADE IN
GERMANY

Mark of grill plate.

Grill plate, 10.75" dia., with fish-roe decorating the dividers of the plate, marked "Willow/Made in Germany." *Courtesy of Joyce & Bill Keenan.* $40-50.

Grill plate, 10.625" dia., Germany. *Courtesy of Joyce & Bill Keenan.* $40-50.

Two creamers. *Left:* 3" h., marked "Société Céramique/Maestricht/Made in Holland/ Willow." *Right:* 2.75" h., England, c. 1891+. *Courtesy of Joyce & Bill Keenan.* $35-50; $45-60.

Oval platter, 13.75" x 11", marked "Arklow Classics/Made in Ireland." *Courtesy of Joyce & Bill Keenan.* $75-100.

Mark of platter.

Detail.

Grill plate, 10.5" dia., marked "Made in Poland." *Courtesy of Joyce & Bill Keenan.* $40-50.

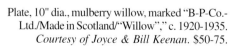

Mark of plate.

Plate, 10" dia., mulberry willow, marked "B-P-Co.-Ltd./Made in Scotland/"Willow"," c. 1920-1935. *Courtesy of Joyce & Bill Keenan.* $50-75.

Collecting Sets or Specialized Willow

In addition to the various colors in which willow is available, there are many other interesting aspects of the pattern that intrigue collectors, causing some to focus portions of their collection on a specific pattern, pattern variation, or type of willow. If you are in search of a way to focus or specialize your collection or wish to branch out into other avenues of willow collectibles, a look into some of these more unique types of willow may give you some fresh ideas. This example of restaurant ware decorated in the willow pattern appeals to willow collectors not only for its display of the willow pattern, but for its significance in the field of commercial wares as a whole. Denser and thicker in quality, more utilitarian in style, and very functional and durable in make, commercial wares were produced for use by restaurants, hotels, railroad and steamship companies, hospitals, military and naval academies, governmental agencies, and other private and public institutions (Altman 140).

Other collectors of willow may find commemorative or advertising pieces decorated in the willow pattern of particular interest. The two tips trays are a good example of advertising pieces in the willow pattern. Bearing the advertiser's name, pieces such as these may have been given away as promotional items or used by establishments to endorse specific products or commercial firms. They were also manufactured for merchants, religious institutions, and civic groups, and to commemorate buildings, places, and organizations (Altman 63). They retain value as novelty items, in addition to their value as willow collectibles.

Looking for sets of willow that can be purchased together or acquired over time can also help a collector branch out or specialize in a particular area. The McCoy pottery cookie jar with matching creamer and sugar and the Homer Laughlin Fiesta Kitchen Kraft Ovenserve line are two possible sets of willow available to collectors. Collectors may spot a piece due to its unusual display of the pattern, its shape, or its size only to discover years later that the piece is part of a set. Wash sets as well as coffee and tea, child's, and syrup and batter sets can also be found decorated in the willow pattern. Sets of willow in unusual multicolor and variant patterns prove particularly striking.

Individually or in sets, Gaudy Willow is a welcome departure from traditional blue and white willow, and very appealing and eye-catching due to its multicolored, hand decorations, known as clobbering. Gaudy Willow required more time to produce than conventional blue and white wares, as various colors—rust, deep blue, pure coin gold, and varying shades of greens and browns—were applied by hand both over and under the glaze as a form of embellishment. Today, this type of willow ware is limited in availability and very collectible. Buffalo Pottery Co. is the only company known to have produced this type of willow in America. (Altman 34)

Pekin willow is another multicolor, variant pattern available in sets or individually. It can be found with a variety of colored backgrounds such as ivory, black, green, and shades of blues and reds. Some of the background color variations are rarer than others. Some pieces may also appear trimmed in gold. Searching for Pekin with a particular background color may prove quite an endeavor, or may be just the challenge you're looking for! In your search for willow, look for pieces that complete a set you've already started or complementary pieces that you didn't know existed.

Mark of teacup.

Small dish or saucer and handleless teacup, pink willow, restaurant ware, by Jackson China Co., Falls Creek, Pennsylvania, USA. *Courtesy of Joyce & Bill Keenan.* $25-35 set.

Two small tip trays. *Left:* Schweppes, 4.75" dia., marked "Unicorn Tableware/Est 1835/Made in England/Member of the Wedgwood Group." $12-18 (new). *Right:* Schweppes Indian Tonic, 4.75" dia., marked on back Keller Guerin, Luneville, France. $75-100. *Courtesy of Joyce & Bill Keenan.*

Cookie jar in shape of coffee pot, 8.75" h., with creamer and sugar, both 5" h., by Nelson McCoy Pottery Company, Roseville, Ohio, USA, c. 1911+. *Courtesy of Joyce & Bill Keenan.* Cookie jar: $75-100; creamer/sugar: $25-35 pair.

Set of nesting mixing bowls, Fiesta Kitchen Kraft with Chinese willow pattern, by Homer Laughlin China Co., East Liverpool, Ohio, USA, marked Kitchen Kraft on bottom, mid-1937. *Courtesy of Tim & Kim Allen.* $125-150 for set.

Note: Kitchen Kraft was a New Ovenserve line developed in 1937 by Homer Laughlin China Co., of East Liverpool, Ohio, USA (Cunningham, 1998 131).

Large bowl from set, pictured alone to show detail of Chinese willow pattern. *Courtesy of Tim & Kim Allen.*

Pair of covered casserole dishes, part of Fiesta Kitchen Kraft set. *Left*: 3" h., 7.75" dia. *Right*: 3.25" h., 8.5" dia. According to company records, only one in 100 casseroles were made with a lid. *Courtesy of Tim & Kim Allen.* $125-150 each.

Large covered jug, missing lid, 5.25" h., part of Fiesta Kitchen Kraft set. *Courtesy of Tim & Kim Allen.* $60-85 without lid; $100-115 with lid.

Gaudy Willow

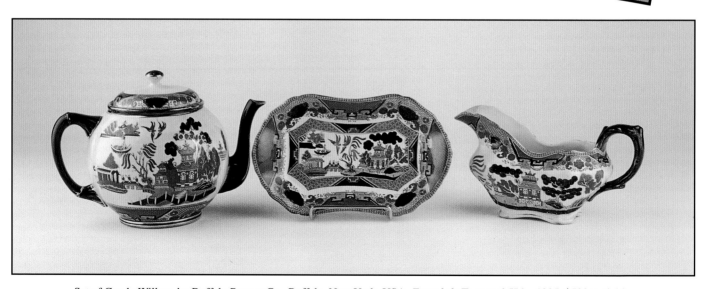

Set of Gaudy Willow, by Buffalo Pottery Co., Buffalo, New York, USA. *From left*: Teapot, 6.5" h., 1905, $500+; pickle dish, 4.5 h. x 8" l., 1908, $250+; gravy boat, 3" h. x 7.5" l., 1908, $275+. *Courtesy of Tim & Kim Allen.*

Pekin pattern

Assortment of Pekin patterned willow, with black background, Royal Winton, by Grimwades Ltd., Stoke, England, c. 1951+, Godden's #1838. *From left*: Milk jug, 4.5" h., $100-125; sugar, 1.25" h., and creamer, 2.5" h., $100-125 pair. *Courtesy of Tim & Kim Allen.*

Salad fork and spoon, 9" l., Pekin pattern, with black background, unmarked. *Courtesy of Michael L. Curtner.* $275-300 set.

Also part of set: pin dish or tray, 3" x 4.25", with teacup and saucer (cup: 3" h). *Courtesy of Tim & Kim Allen.* Pin dish/tray: $75-100; teacup/saucer: $90-125 pair.

Creamer, 3.25" h., and ash tray, 2.75 x 3.5" (from smoking set), Pekin pattern, with green background, Royal Winton, by Grimwades Ltd., Stoke, England, marked "J-W.Co. Staffordshire England Royal Winton," c. 1930+. *Courtesy of Tim & Kim Allen.* Creamer: $100-125; ash tray: $45-55.

Demitasse cup, 2.5" h., and salad plate, 7.75" sq., Pekin pattern, with red background (cup) and burgundy background (plate), Royal Winton, by Grimwades Ltd., Stoke, England, c. 1951+, Godden's #1838. *Courtesy of Tim & Kim Allen.* Cup: $40-50; plate: $75-90.

One from a series of plates by Doulton & Co., Burslem, England, impressed date of 1911. (This is #2 in the series.) Each plate depicts a part of the willow legend. Other plates in series are shown in the medallions around the perimeter of plate. 10.5" dia. (Series is also known to be found in sepia, mauve and black, and other polychrome variations. It is rare to see a complete set.) *Courtesy of Tim & Kim Allen.* $200-250 (for a single plate).

Details of medallions around perimeter of plate. Each depict a part of the willow legend.

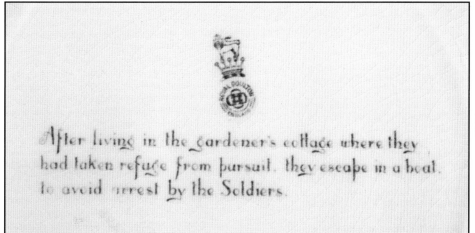

After living in the gardener's cottage where they had taken refuge from pursuit, they escape in a boat, to avoid arrest by the Soldiers.

Back of plate, #2 in series.

Chapter One
Plates

Because the willow pattern originated in England during the late eighteenth to early nineteenth century, the earliest examples of willow-patterned wares are of English manufacture. Many of the early manufacturers, however, were not in the habit of marking their wares; thus, unless marked, it is very difficult to determine the manufacturer, date, and place of origin of early willow items. Records of the factories producing willow, the patterns they used, the wares they made, etc. were simply not kept or, in the rare instance that records did at one time exist, they have since been lost or destroyed.

Pearlware plates and other items offer some of the earliest examples of the willow pattern produced using the methods of blue transfer printing. Introduced and first marketed by Josiah Wedgwood as "Pearl White," circa 1779, pearlware was a more durable and affordable ware than its predecessors. Its white earthenware body was composed of a mixture of white clay and flint, to which small amounts of cobalt were added. For use as tableware, a colorless glaze was applied to the surface of the ware and the methods of transfer-printing were often employed in the decoration of the ware (Hughes 121). To distinguish pearlware from other wares, more specifically creamware, look at the coloring: there tends to be a bluish-white tint to the glaze of pearlware where in other wares there is not. (On creamware items the glaze appears to have a yellow or green tint (Hume 129-130). Another distinguishing quality is that pearlware from 1840 can be found impressed with the name "Pearl," while items circa 1868 are marked with the letter "P" (Godden xxi).

During the early 1800s, pearlware was the most widely used kind of earthenware, and was the dominant ware on the American market in 1810. Considering the widespread popularity of the willow pattern during the turn from the eighteenth to nineteenth century, it is reasonable to assume that a fair number of the pearlware items manufactured during that time were decorated in the willow pattern. (However, finding these items may prove to be another matter.)

English

Plate, 9.75" dia., pearlware, England, marked with "I" on back, c. 1810. Note the split tail birds in pattern. *Courtesy of J. Dennis Crosby.* $100-125.

Plate, 10" dia., pearlware, England, marked "W P" above "Staffordshire Stone China," c. 1810. *Courtesy of J. Dennis Crosby.* $100-125.

Mark of plate.

Plate, 8.5" dia., pearlware, England, unmarked, c. 1810. *Courtesy of J. Dennis Crosby*. $75-100.

Plate, 8.5" dia., pearlware, England, unmarked, c. 1810. *Courtesy of J. Dennis Crosby*. $75-100.

Plate, 9.75" dia., pearlware, England, impressed on back with "H," c. 1810. *Courtesy of J. Dennis Crosby*. $100-125.

Mark of plate.

Plate, 10.25" dia., by Thomas Walker, Tunstall, England, marked "T.W." below "Stone Ware" and impressed with Godden's #3982a, c. 1845-1851. *Courtesy of J. Dennis Crosby*. $100-125.

Mark of plate, also showing "Crook/Motcomb St. Belgrave/ London," the distributor's mark.

Plate, 10" dia., Two Temples I pattern, originally heavily gilded, by W. T. Copeland, Stoke, England, c. 1875-1890, Godden's #1074. Note the butterfly border. *Courtesy of Tim & Kim Allen*. $75-100.

Mark of plate.

Plate, 10" dia., black transfer print with mustard glaze, by Doulton & Co., Burslem, England, c. 1891-1902, Godden's #1332. *Courtesy of Tim & Kim Allen.* $150-175.

Mark of plate.

Plate, 9.75" dia., by Wedgwood & Co., Ltd., England, after 1900. *Courtesy of J. Dennis Crosby.* $50-65.

Mark of grill plate.

Grill plate, 9.875" dia., with raised scalloped edge, by J. Kent Ltd., Fenton, England, c. 1913+, Godden's #2267. *Courtesy of Joyce & Bill Keenan.* $35-50.

Mark of bread plate.

Bread plate (or breakfast plate), 8" dia., by S. Hancock & Sons, Stoke-on-Trent, England, c. 1912-1937. Note the variation in the border—fish-roe on inside, and scroll and flower on outside. *Courtesy of Joyce & Bill Keenan.* $25-35.

Grill plate, 10.375" dia., by Elijah Cotton, Hanley, England, marked "BCM/Nelson Ware/Made in England," c. 1932. *Courtesy of Joyce & Bill Keenan.* $15-20.

Grill plate, 10.875" dia., by John Steventon & Sons Ltd., Burslem, England, c. 1923-1936. *Courtesy of Joyce & Bill Keenan.* $15-20.

Mark of grill plate.

Grill plate, 11.25" dia., marked "Rowland and Marsellus/Made in England." *Courtesy of Joyce & Bill Keenan.* $15-20.

Plate, 8" dia., by Wedgwood & Co. Ltd., England, c. 1938+. *Courtesy of Joyce & Bill Keenan.* $15-20.

Mark of bread plate.

Bread plate, 6.75" dia., by Washington Pottery Ltd., Shelton, England, c. 1946-1973. *Courtesy of Joyce & Bill Keenan.* $10-15.

Detail of unknown
impressed mark.

Plate, 9.5" dia., England, unknown
impressed mark on back. *Courtesy of J.
Dennis Crosby.* $35-40.

Plate, 10" dia., England.
Courtesy of J. Dennis Crosby.
$15-20.

Plate, 10" dia., by George Phillips, Longport, England, c. 1834-1848. Unusual due to small number 2 that appears at entrance near bridge. *Courtesy of J. Dennis Crosby.* $75-100.

Detail, showing small number 2 that appears at entrance near bridge.

Mark of plate.

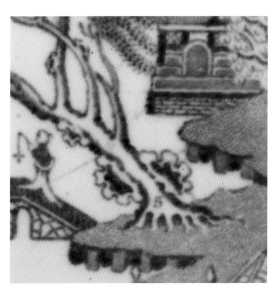

Detail, showing small number 5 that appears at base of tree.

Plate, 9" dia., England. Unusual due to small number 5 that appears at base of tree. *Courtesy of J. Dennis Crosby.* $75-100.

Plate, 9" dia., semi-porcelain, variant pattern, England, c. early- to mid-1800s. *Courtesy of Joyce & Bill Keenan.* $50-75.

Plate, 8 sided, 6.75" dia., porcelain, 'calico' willow pattern, unmarked though attributed to Adderleys Ltd., Longton, England, c. 1876-1905. *Courtesy of Tim & Kim Allen*. $60-75.

Note: 'Calico' willow is a generalized term used to refer to items decorated with an overall monochrome repeating sheet transfer pattern, and thus appears in quotations throughout the text.

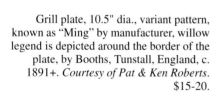

Grill plate, 10.5" dia., variant pattern, known as "Ming" by manufacturer, willow legend is depicted around the border of the plate, by Booths, Tunstall, England, c. 1891+. *Courtesy of Pat & Ken Roberts*. $15-20.

Grill plate, 10.875" dia., by G.L. Ashworth Bros., Hanley, England, c. 1891-1900, Godden's #147. $45-60.

Grill plate, 12.75" dia., Canton variant pattern, by G.L. Ashworth Bros., Hanley, England, c. 1891-1900, Godden's #147. *Courtesy of Joyce & Bill Keenan.* $50-75.

In America, the Buffalo Pottery Co., of Buffalo, New York, was the first manufacturer to refine the techniques of transfer printing for use in the decoration of willow-patterned wares. Before 1905, American manufacturers were not able to achieve the quality of effects that the English manufacturers were in using the methods of blue transfer printing; however, through the efforts of William J. Rea, the first superintendent of production at Buffalo Pottery, methods to reproduce the willow pattern underglaze were refined, and the wares that resulted proved to be of a quality comparable, perhaps even superior, to that of the English-made, imported willow. The Buffalo Pottery Co. (whose name was changed to Buffalo China in 1915) is honored as the "originators of old blue willow in the United States," and the wares are marked as the first willow manufactured in America. Items marked "Buffalo Pottery" are more desirable than those marked "Buffalo China," as this change in mark reflects an item's age, and pieces marked "First Old Willow Ware Manufactured in America" and dated 1905 are valued most highly for their age. Other American manufacturers eventually acquired the means to produce blue transfer-printed willow as well as willow through other methods, such as decalcomania and rubber stamping. Royal China and Homer Laughlin are two examples of other American companies that have produced an abundance of willow-patterned wares. (Altman 19, 21, 28, 33; Allen, *handout*)

American

Grill plate, 9.75" dia., by Wellsville China Company, Wellsville, Ohio, USA, c. 1902-1959 (69). *Courtesy of Joyce & Bill Keenan.* $12-18.

Grill plate, 9.75" dia., by Shenango China Co., New Castle, Pennsylvania, USA, c. 1915-1940. Note: The pattern on the plate is the Turner pattern with scroll and flower border. *Courtesy of Joyce & Bill Keenan.* $20-30.

Mark of plate.

Grill plate, 10.625" dia., by Buffalo Pottery Co., Buffalo, New York, USA, c. 1915+. *Courtesy of Joyce & Bill Keenan.* $25-35.

Bread and butter plate, 6" dia., Two Temples II pattern, by Limoges China Co., Sebring, Ohio, USA, c. 1924, Lehner's #43. *Courtesy of Tim & Kim Allen.* $5-10.

Bread and butter plate, 6" dia., variant decal, attributed to W.S. George, USA, c. 1930s. *Courtesy of Tim & Kim Allen.* $5-10.

Plate, 9.25" dia., traditional center pattern with no border, by Royal China Co., Sebring, Ohio, USA, c. 1930s-1940s. *Courtesy of Joyce & Bill Keenan.* $8-10.

Plate, 8.25" dia., Hope willow, by Ostrow China (formerly Hopewell China), Hopewell, Virginia, USA, marked "English Brambleberry," c. 1935-1938. *Courtesy of Tim & Kim Allen.* $25-40.

Plate, 10" dia., Two Temples II reversed pattern, by Edwin M. Knowles China Co., Newell, West Virginia, (offices located in East Liverpool, Ohio), USA, March 1942, Lehner's #4. *Courtesy of Tim & Kim Allen.* $10-12.

Saucer, 5.75" dia., variant decal, by Homer Laughlin China Co., East Liverpool, Ohio, USA, 1946. *Courtesy of Tim & Kim Allen.* $4-8.

Bread and butter plate, 6.25" dia., Two Temples II reversed pattern, in gold, USA. *Courtesy of Tim & Kim Allen.* $6-10.

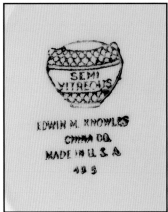

Plate, 7.25" dia., Two Temples II reversed pattern with Bridal Gold #2 border pattern, in gold, by Edwin M. Knowles China Co., Newell, West Virginia, USA, 1949. *Courtesy of Tim & Kim Allen.* $6-10.

Plate, 10" dia., opaque white glass, advertised as "Platonite" by manufacturer, though unmarked attributed to Hazel-Atlas Glass Company, Clarksville, West Virginia, USA. *Courtesy of Joyce & Bill Keenan.* $18-25.

Two grill plates, 9.5" dia., both marked "Denver/Grill Plate/Made in U.S.A." (Denver indicative of shape), probably 1950s+. *Left: Courtesy of Joyce & Bill Keenan. Below: Courtesy of Tim & Kim Allen.* Blue: $60-70; green: $70-80.

Note: Both grill plates have four divided sections instead of three, perhaps used to serve club sandwiches.

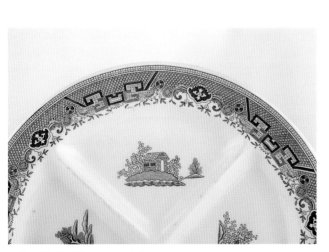

Detail of grill plate on right.

Unusual four-part grill plate, 10" dia., unmarked though identical plate seen marked "Shenango China New Castle, Pa.," USA, probably c. 1950s+. *Courtesy of Tim & Kim Allen.* $45-60.

Detail of largest section of grill plate.

Grill plate, 9.5" dia., medallion of willow pattern in each section of plate, by Jackson China Co., Falls Creek, Pennsylvania, USA, c. 1960s. *Courtesy of Joyce & Bill Keenan.* $15-20.

Grill plate, 9.5" dia., by Jackson China Co., Falls Creek, Pennsylvania, USA, c. 1960s. *Courtesy of Joyce & Bill Keenan.* $12-15.

Plate, 9.625" dia., hotel and restaurant ware, by Homer Laughlin China Co., East Liverpool, Ohio, USA, c. mid-1970s. *Courtesy of Joyce & Bill Keenan.* $15-20.

On the Japanese market, willow ware was produced by Japanese manufacturers mostly for the purpose of export to help boost the economy. However, identifying the specific manufacturer of a Japanese-made item is much less likely than for items of American or English origin. Often Japanese-made items were not marked with the company name, and many of the company records, which may have provided a lead to the company's line of production and years of operation, were destroyed during World War II. Also, wares made after WWII were marked with only paper labels, which were deliberately removed when the items were distributed on the foreign market or easily fell off. If items are marked, "Japan," "Made in Japan," "Occupied Japan," "Made in Occupied Japan," or other wording similar to these is all that will usually appear. Items marked "Nippon" are also of Japanese origin. (Prior to the early twentieth century, Japan was known as Nippon.) More than likely Nippon items date between the years 1891 and 1921. (Allen, *handout*)

Typical Japanese-made willow features the traditional pattern, with perhaps small alterations to some of the elements; many Japanese factories are known to have used the same transfer-printed design or decal. A chubbier, plumper depiction of the birds in the pattern, referred to as "Fatbirds," may be an indication of an item's Japanese origin. "Double Phoenix" also appears in the mark of many Japanese-made items decorated in the Booths (willow) pattern.

Japanese

Grill plate, 10" dia., marked "Made in Japan." Note the appearance of four birds in top right section of plate. *Courtesy of Joyce & Bill Keenan.* $15-18.

Detail of four birds in upper right section of plate.

Mark of plate.

Mark of plate.

Grill plate, 10.813" dia., by Moriyama, marked "Made in Japan." *Courtesy of Joyce & Bill Keenan.* $25-35.

Grill plate, 9.875" dia., Japan. Note: The pattern on the plate is Two Temples II reversed with two birds and a boat. *Courtesy of Joyce & Bill Keenan.* $12-15.

Plate, 10" dia., by NKT (or Nihon Koshitsu Toki Company), Japan, marked "Double Phoenix" by manufacturer. *Courtesy of Tim & Kim Allen*. $20-25.

Saucer, 7.5" dia., variant pattern, marked "Mandarin Blue by Maruta, Japan." *Courtesy of Joyce & Bill Keenan*. $4-6.

The diversity and multiplicity of color involved in the polychrome or multicolor pieces of willow bring astonishment to collectors who unknowingly assume willow to mean just blue and white! Early on, colors were applied to a ware by hand over the glaze. Later, manufacturers developed the means to apply color under the glaze. In 1848, F. Collins and A. Reynolds, in Hanley, England, introduced the use of a variety of colors—blue, red, and yellow—in underglaze printing, adding the colors brown and green, later, in 1852 (Hughes 151). Another method known as clobbering also allowed for the manufacture of willow in multicolor variations. In clobbering, enamel colors are added overglaze (after the application of the transfer-printed design) as a form of embellishment. The effect produces a ware of many colors where the transfer-printed design (underglaze) is still apparent (Hughes

46). In the US, the Buffalo Pottery Co. was the first company to produce a multicolored underglaze version of the willow pattern, known as Gaudy Willow (see page 6 and 35 for further information on Gaudy Willow).

Polychrome examples display much experimentation not only in the use of colors, but also in the depiction of the various elements of the willow pattern and border designs, as well as unusual modifications to the pattern's overall appearance. As a result, some polychrome willow variants just barely contain the elements deemed characteristic of the willow pattern. Some controversy exists as to what variants may or may not be regarded as within the constraints of the willow family. Regardless, many collectors take to the polychrome variants for the sheer joy of their beauty and unique appearance.

Multicolored, Variants, & Rarities

Plate, 10" dia., traditional center pattern, with brown inner border and surrounding variant border, known as "Manchu" pattern by manufacturer, by Alfred Meakin, Tunstall, England, c. 1891-1930. *Courtesy of Tim & Kim Allen.* $25-30.

Mark of plate.

Plate, 10.5" dia., center willow pattern, with unusual floral border motif and embossed edge, hand painted underglaze, by Mason's, England, c. 1885. *Courtesy of Charles & Louise Loehr, Louise's Old Things.* $200-250.

Plate, 9" dia., unusual, traditional pattern with overpainting, also known as clobbering, marked "Made in England." *Courtesy of Tim & Kim Allen.* $75-100.

Grill plate, 10.625" dia., Davenport Willow pattern with overpainting, also known as clobbering, by Booths, Tunstall, England, c. 1906+, Godden's #453. *Courtesy of Joyce & Bill Keenan*. $75-100.

Note: Clobbering is a technique for decorating ceramic wares that involves hand painting over a transfer printed design (Roberts 154).

Plate, 9" dia., unusual, Worcester pattern with overpainting, also known as clobbering, by A.G.Harley Jones, Fenton, England, marked "Wilton Ware" by manufacturer, c. 1923-1934, Godden's #2212. *Courtesy of Tim & Kim Allen*. $75-100.

Mark of plate.

Grill plate, 10.375" dia., Two temples II reversed pattern, clobbered, Japan. *Courtesy of Joyce & Bill Keenan*. $30-40.

Plate, 10" dia., yellow transfer print, clobbered with gold detailing, by Wedgwood, England, marked "Wedgwood/ Etruria, England," and impressed "ATF" and "Wedgwood," April 1903. *Courtesy of Tim & Kim Allen*. $125-150.

Mark of plate.

Mark of plate.

Plate, 9.5" dia., transfer print with overpainting, also known as clobbering, by G.M. & C.J. Mason, Hanley, England, c. 1820, Kovel's #94c. Note the use of Turner center pattern with scroll and flower border. *Courtesy of Tim & Kim Allen.* $100-125.

Plate, 10.25" dia., variant pattern, transfer print with overpainting, also known as clobbering, unmarked though attributed to G.L. Ashworth & Bros., Hanley, England, c. 1862+. *Courtesy of Tim & Kim Allen.* $75-100.

Mark of plate.

Plate, 10" dia., Gaudy Willow, by Buffalo
Pottery Co., Buffalo, New York, USA, 1907.
Courtesy of Tim & Kim Allen. $200+.

Plate, 7" dia., porcelain, transfer print with
overpainting, also known as clobbering, by Samuel
Radford Ltd., Fenton, England, c. 1891+, Godden's
#3184 with "England" above crown. *Courtesy of Tim
& Kim Allen.* $125-150.

Mark of plate.

Mark of plate.

Plate, 7.75" dia., variant pattern, transfer print with overpainting, also known as clobbering, G. L. Ashworth & Bros., Hanley, England, c. 1862, Godden's #146 and impressed "Ashworth's Real Ironstone China." Note how the border combines many motifs, recognizable among them are elements from the butterfly, scroll and flower, floral, and traditional willow borders. *Courtesy of Tim & Kim Allen.* $60-75.

Plate, 9.5" dia., brown transfer print with overpainting, also known as clobbering, England. Note: The pattern on the plate is Two Temples II with butterfly border. *Courtesy of Tim & Kim Allen.* $75-100.

Mark of plate.

Plate, 9.75" dia., multicolor Two Temples II decal, also referred to as Parrott pattern, known as "Pagoda" pattern by manufacturer, by Davison & Sons Ltd., Burslem, England, c. 1898-1952. *Courtesy of Tim & Kim Allen.* $50-65.

Mark of plate.

Plate, 10.25" dia., variant pattern, by British Art Pottery Co. Ltd., Fenton, England, c. 1920-1926. *Courtesy of Tim & Kim Allen.* $50-75.

Mark of plate. (Note the word Willow is not usually present, but refers here to the pattern name.)

Plate, 9.75" dia., variant pattern with overpainting, also known as clobbering, by Keeling & Co. Ltd., Burslem, England, impressed "11-28," 1928, Godden's #2245 with "Willow" added above crown. *Courtesy of Tim & Kim Allen.* $65-80.

Plate, 7.5" dia., traditional decal with gold trim on edges, by Lancaster & Sandland Ltd., Hanley, England, c. 1949+, Godden's #2328. *Courtesy of Tim & Kim Allen.* $35-45.

Mark of plate.

Octagonal plate, 10.375" dia., variant decal with wide pink border, by Empire Porcelain Co. (Ltd.), Stoke, England, May 1925, Godden's #1490. *Courtesy of Tim & Kim Allen.* $60-75.

Plate, 8.5" dia., bone china, floral variant pattern, known as "Manchu" pattern by manufacturer, by Royal Paragon, England. *Courtesy of Tim & Kim Allen.* $50-60.

Mark of plate.

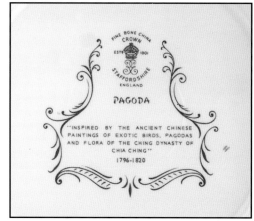

Mark of plate.

Plate, 8.25" dia., bone china, floral variant pattern, known as "Pagoda" pattern by manufacturer, by Crown Staffordshire Porcelain Co. Ltd., Fenton, England, c. 1906+, Godden's #1149. Note the incorporation of willow elements—birds, temple, bridge with figures, and boat—in combination with the overall floral motif. *Courtesy of Tim & Kim Allen.* $35-45.

Plate, 8.25" dia., variant decal with floral motif, known as "Manchu" pattern by manufacturer, by Wedgwood & Co. Ltd., Tunstall, England, c. 1908+, Godden's #4061 with "Manchu" pattern name. *Courtesy of Tim & Kim Allen.* $35-50.

Mark of plate.

Plate, 6" dia., probably porcelain, Two Temples II pattern, gold transfer print on mottled blue body with enamel detailing, by E. Hughes & Co., Fenton, England, c. 1930-1941, Godden's #2120 with "China" in middle instead of "Fenton." *Courtesy of Tim & Kim Allen*. $75-100.

Dinner plate, 10" dia., Pekin pattern, with black background, Royal Winton, by Grimwades Ltd., Stoke, England, c. 1951+, Godden's #1838. *Courtesy of Tim & Kim Allen*. $75-100.

Mark of plate.

Octagonal plate, 8.5" dia., chintz, England.
Courtesy of Tim & Kim Allen. $75-100.

Plate, 10" dia., traditional decal, by Elijah Cotton,
Hanley, England, marked "C. M./ Nelson Ware,
Made in England" and impressed "8\30," c. 1930.
Courtesy of Tim & Kim Allen. $35-40.

Plate, 8.5" dia., hand painted decoration over a matte
black background, Basaltine willow, by Frank Beardmore
& Co., Fenton, England, 1903-1914, Godden's #307a.
Courtesy of Tim & Kim Allen. $125-150.

Note: It is supposed that the term 'Basaltine' may be
derived from the item's basalt-like finish (IWC convention catalog, VI, 1998).

Plate, 7.75" dia., hand painted multicolor
pattern, Occupied Japan. *Courtesy of Tim
& Kim Allen.* $35-50.

Plate, 6.25" dia., porcelain, hand painted
enamel on matte black background, variant
pattern, by Noritake, Japan, marked
"Noritake" plus "M" in circle with wreath,
c. post-1904. *Courtesy of Tim & Kim Allen.*
$45-60.

Plate, 10.25" dia., variant pattern with
bird and floral medallion-like border motif,
by G. L. Ashworth & Bros., Hanley,
England, c. 1880+, Godden's #147.
Courtesy of Tim & Kim Allen. $35-50.

Mark of plate.

Plate, 9" dia., porcelain, "Chinese Willow" pattern, by Crown Staffordshire Porcelain Co. Ltd., Fenton, England, c. 1906+, Godden's #1149. *Courtesy of Tim & Kim Allen.* $60-75.

Mark of plate.

Mark of plate.

Plate, 10.5" dia., flow blue, known as "Willow and Aster" pattern by manufacturer pattern, by Doulton & Co., Burslem, England, c. 1891-1902, Godden's #1332 with "Willow and Aster" underneath. *Courtesy of Tim & Kim Allen*. $125-150.

Soup plate, 9.5" dia., flow blue, Persian Spray with willow and aster medallions, by Doulton & Co., Burslem, England, c. 1882-1890, impressed with Godden's #1329. *Courtesy of Tim & Kim Allen*. $125-150.

Note: When the "Willow and Aster" pattern appears without the round willow motif, it is known as "Persian Spray" (IWC convention catalog, VI, 1998).

Depression Era Willow on Glass

Plate, 9.75" dia., opaque white glass, advertised as "Platonite" by manufacturer, Moderntone, with willow center decal in red, red line border, by Hazel-Atlas Glass Company, Clarksville, West Virginia, USA, c. 1938-1956. *Courtesy of Tim & Kim Allen.* $35-50.

Plate, 8" dia., willow pattern etched in glass, by Cambridge Glass Company, Cambridge, Ohio, USA, c. 1920s-1930s. *Courtesy of Tim & Kim Allen.* $50-65.

Detail of pattern etched in glass.

Plate, 8" dia., willow pattern etched in glass with enamel fill, by Cambridge Glass Company, Cambridge, Ohio, USA, c. 1920s-1930s. *Courtesy of Tim & Kim Allen*. $50-65.

Plate, 10.5" dia., willow pattern etched in glass from front and gold encrusted, by Cambridge Glass Company, Cambridge, Ohio, USA, c. 1920s-1930s. *Courtesy of Tim & Kim Allen*. $125-150.

Detail of pattern etched in glass with enamel fill.

Detail of pattern etched in glass from front and gold encrusted.

Chapter Two
Serving Pieces

Flatware

Mark of rectangular platter.

Rectangular platter, 11" x 13.75", by John Meir & Son, Tunstall, England, c. 1837-1897. *Courtesy of Joyce & Bill Keenan.* $150-175.

Rectangular platter with well and tree, 15.25" x 19.75", England, c. 1840-1860. *Courtesy of Joyce & Bill Keenan.* Note: The well and tree design of the platter allowed for the juices from the meat to drain and collect in the well at the bottom of the plate. $350-500.

Mark of platter, showing impressed anchor.

Rectangular platter, 17.25" x 13.875", by Davenport, Longport, England, Davenport mark with impressed anchor, c. 1820+. *Courtesy of Joyce & Bill Keenan.* $225-275.

Rectangular platter, 10" x 7.5", reticulated, England, c. mid-1800s. *Courtesy of Joyce & Bill Keenan.* $250-295.

Drainer (designed to sit on top of a platter to allow juices to drain), 8.75" x 12.25", England. *Courtesy of Joyce & Bill Keenan.* $200-250.

Hot water plate, 2" h., 10" dia., attributed to Wood & Challinor, Tunstall, England, marked with WC in Staffordshire bowknot, c. 1828-1843. Plates such as this one can also be found with a tin bottom. According to one source, it is more unusual to find one with a ceramic bottom and spout as the one pictured here. *Courtesy of J. Dennis Crosby.* $200-250.

Front view of hot water plate.

Detail of side of hot water plate, showing underneath of spout and hole that may have held chain for cork.

Mark of hot water plate.

Oval platter, 13" dia., continuous pictorial inner border and traditional outer border, unmarked though attributed to Grafton China, A. B. Jones & Sons, Longton, England, c. 1930+. *Courtesy of Tim & Kim Allen.* $75-95.

Footed fruit compote or possible cheese dish, 3" h., 9.75" dia., England, c. 1840s. It is assumed that the rim of this dish would have been used for the deposit of fruit pits. *Courtesy of Shirley & James Hillier.* $275-300.

Alternate view of compote showing footed base.

Cheese stand or dish, 3" h., 10" dia., England, c. 1830. *Courtesy of Tim & Kim Allen.* $275-300.

Pedestal base cheese platter, 9.5" dia., England, c. early 1800s. *Courtesy of Joyce & Bill Keenan.* $275-300.

Alternate view showing top of cheese platter.

Cheese dish with cover, 6.5" x 7.75" (dish), 3" h. (cover), England, c. 1891+. *Courtesy of Joyce & Bill Keenan.* $175-225.

Small rectangular platter (maybe from a child's set) or undertray for sauce tureen, 5.5" x 7.25", England. *Courtesy of Joyce & Bill Keenan.* $75-100.

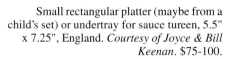

Oval platter, 14.875" x 11", by Gibson & Sons, Burslem, England, c. 1912+. *Courtesy of Joyce & Bill Keenan.* $65-75.

Handled serving plate, 10.125" x 9.125", Turner center pattern with scroll and flower border, by Mason's, England, c. 1891+. *Courtesy of Joyce & Bill Keenan.* $60-75.

Mark of above plate.

Round snack plate with cup rest, 9.25" dia., by Royal China Co., USA, c. 1930s-1940s. *Courtesy of Joyce & Bill Keenan.* $20-30 without cup; $25-35 with cup.

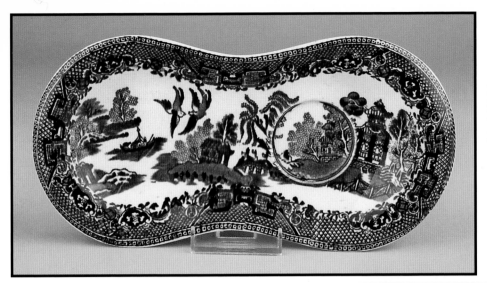

Figure 8 snack plate with cup rest, 9.375" x 4.625", by Grimwades Ltd., Stoke, England, c. 1930+. *Courtesy of Joyce & Bill Keenan*. $50-60 without cup; $75-95 with cup.

Oval platter, 15" x 18.625", by Wood & Sons, Burslem, England, marked "Willow/Woods Ware/Wood & Sons/England" and impressed "WI30 91," c. 1917+. *Courtesy of Joyce & Bill Keenan*. $100-125.

Mark of platter.

Oval serving dish, 6.625" x 8.625", pink willow, by Wood & Sons, Burslem, England, c. 1917-1930. *Courtesy of Joyce & Bill Keenan*. $35-50.

Rectangular platter, 8" x 9.75", pink willow, by Newport Pottery Co. Ltd., Burslem, England, c. 1920-1937. *Courtesy of Joyce & Bill Keenan.* $75-100.

Mark of platter.

Oval platter, 8" x 10.375", with scalloped edge, pink willow, by Swinnertons Ltd., Hanley, England, c. 1930-1946. *Courtesy of Joyce & Bill Keenan.* $40-60.

Oval serving dish, 7" x 9.125", with scalloped edge, pink willow, by Swinnertons Ltd., Hanley, England, c. 1930-1946. *Courtesy of Joyce & Bill Keenan.* $40-60.

Oval platter, 11.75" x 8.5", with scalloped edge, Mandarin pattern with dagger border, known as "Ching" pattern by manufacturer, by Samuel Alcock & Co., Cobridge, England, c. 1828-1859. *Courtesy of Joyce & Bill Keenan.* $75-100.

Footed compote, 3.25" h., 6" dia., elements of willow pattern decorate perimeter of top, by Hall China Co., East Liverpool, Ohio, USA, c. 1930s, Lehner's #1. *Courtesy of Joyce & Bill Keenan.* $65-75.

Oval asparagus plate (or undertray for soup/sauce tureen), 9" x 6.75", by John & William Ridgway, Hanley, England, c. pre-1891. *Courtesy of Joyce & Bill Keenan.* $60-75.

Alternate view showing top only.

Oval platter, 11.25" x 15.25", by Hopewell China, Hopewell, Virginia, USA, October 1924. *Courtesy of Joyce & Bill Keenan*. $45-60.

Footed compote, 4 h., 8.5 dia, with scalloped edge, rare, black 'calico' willow center pattern with daisy border in blue, by William Alsager Adderley, Longton, England, 1876-1885. *Courtesy of Tom & Barbara Allen*. $375-425.

Alternate view of compote.

Mark of compote.

Handled cake plate, 9.5" dia., with two dessert plates, 6" dia., Martha Washington shape, by French China Co., Sebring, Ohio, USA, 1926, Lehner's #9. *Courtesy of Tim & Kim Allen*. $50-75 set.

Plate, 8.75", on original Bakelite stand (glaze extends into hole of stand), transfer print with overpainting, also known as clobbering, by Newport Pottery Company, Ltd., Burslem, England, c. 1920+, Godden's #3876. Note: The willow pattern is in underglaze brown with green, rust, and black overglaze. *Courtesy of Tim & Kim Allen.* $275-300.

Alternate view to show top of plate.

Oval tray, 6.75" x 9.5", bone china, Chinese Legend pattern, by Wedgwood, England, c. 1985-1992. *Courtesy of Tim & Kim Allen.* $100-125.

Child's dinner service (not complete set), England, marked "Shell Ware" by manufacturer, c. early 1900s. *Courtesy of Charles & Louise Loehr, Louise's Old Things.* $375-425 (if complete set).

Hollow Ware

Oval soup tureen with lid, 7.5" x 10.75" x 8", by Hulse, Nixon & Adderley, Longton, England, c. 1853-1869. *Courtesy of Joyce & Bill Keenan.* $500-575.

Oval sauce tureen with lid, 4" x 5.875" x 4.25", England, c. pre-1891. *Courtesy of Joyce & Bill Keenan.* $250-300.

Sauce tureen with lid, 5.5" x 4.5" x 6.5", by Buffalo Pottery Co., Buffalo, New York, USA, 1916. *Courtesy of Joyce & Bill Keenan.* $350-400.

Covered vegetable dish, 8 sided and footed, 7" h., 10" dia., very unusual, by Thomas Walker, Tunstall, England, c. 1845-1851. *Courtesy of Tim & Kim Allen.* $350-400.

Oval vegetable dish with lid, 11" x 8.75", by George Taylor, England, c. pre-1891. *Courtesy of Joyce & Bill Keenan.* $250-300.

Vegetable dish with lid, 6" x 11" x 9.25", by Ridgways, Hanley, England, c. 1891+. *Courtesy of Joyce & Bill Keenan.* $200-250.

Alternate view showing top of lid and interior of dish.

Mark of vegetable dish.

Covered vegetable dish, 3.5" x 9.5" x 7.5", Cypress pattern, by S. F. & Co. B. Ltd., England, c. 1892-1900. *Courtesy of Shirley & James Hillier.* $150-175.

Round covered vegetable dish, 9" dia., by Myott, Son & Co., England, c. 1907+. *Courtesy of Joyce & Bill Keenan.* $175-225.

Oval covered vegetable dish (with sugar and creamer), Hope willow, by Hopewell China Co., Hopewell, Virginia, USA, September 1927, Lehner's #2. (Sugar/creamer: April 1926.) *Courtesy of Tim & Kim Allen.* Dish: $175-225; sugar/creamer: $50-60 pair.

Covered vegetable dish, 9.5" sq., variant pattern, known as "Kang-He" pattern by manufacturer, by Thomas Till & Son, Burslem, England, c. 1922-1928. *Courtesy of Joyce & Bill Keenan.* $150-175.

Round vegetable dish with handles, no lid, 7.5" dia., England, c. 1891+. *Courtesy of Joyce & Bill Keenan.* $75-95 without lid; $225-250 with lid.

Oval vegetable with handles, no lid, 9" x 5.875", by
Grimwades Ltd., Stoke, England, c. 1930-1933.
Courtesy of Joyce & Bill Keenan. $75-95 without lid;
$225-250 with lid.

Oval open vegetable dish, 8.75" l., multicolor border with pictorial willow
medallions (simplified variant pattern), by Taylor, Smith & Taylor, Chester,
West Virginia, USA, 1928, Lehner's #14. Note: According to Harvey Duke,
the dish is known as the Belva shape, which is now not easy to find.
Courtesy of Tim & Kim Allen. $50-65.

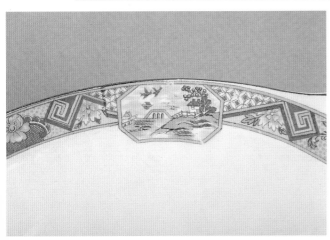

Detail of multicolor border with
pictorial willow medallions.

Mark of oval dish.

Oval dish, 8.5" l., by Gater, Hall & Co., Burslem, England, c. 1914-1943. *Courtesy of Tim & Kim Allen.* $50-75.

Chestnut basket, reticulated, 3.5" h. x 10" l., beautiful, rare example, England, c. 1810. *Courtesy of J. Dennis Crosby.* $750+.

Rectangular dish, 3.25" x 4.375", with scalloped edge and handles, England. *Courtesy of Joyce & Bill Keenan.* $110-175.

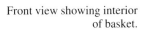

Front view showing interior of basket.

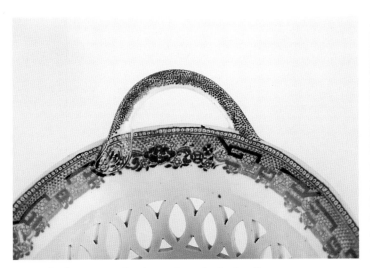

Detail of very unusual under- and over-laying handle.

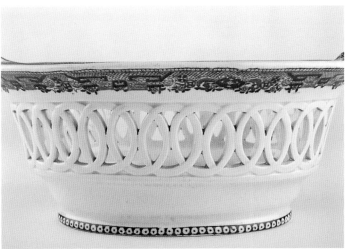

Detail showing reticulated sides of basket.

Round dish with lid, 4" h., 6" dia., by Moriyama, Japan. *Courtesy of Joyce & Bill Keenan*. $75-100.

Round dish with lid, 2.5" h., 3.75" dia., by Moriyama, Japan. *Courtesy of Joyce & Bill Keenan*. $75-100.

Oval dish with lid, 4" x 8.25" x 6", by Moriyama, Japan. *Courtesy of Joyce & Bill Keenan*. $150-175.

Round dish with lid, 1.75" h., 4.125" dia., by Moriyama, Japan. *Courtesy of Joyce & Bill Keenan*. $60-85.

Pair of gravy boats, 2.75" h., 7.75" l., England, c. 1830-1850. *Courtesy of Tim & Kim Allen*. $150-175 each.

Small sauce boat, 3" h., England. *Courtesy of Joyce & Bill Keenan.* $50-65.

Alternate view showing interior of gravy boat.

Gravy boat (unusually shaped), 4" h., Mandarin pattern with dagger border and gold trim, England, c. pre-1891. *Courtesy of Joyce & Bill Keenan.* $60-75.

Egg cup, 2.25" h., by Booths, Tunstall, England, c. 1891+. *Courtesy of Joyce & Bill Keenan.* $35-50.

Potted meat dish, 2.25" h., 5" dia., Parrott pattern, with trowl/spreader and wooden holder, by Newport Pottery Co. Ltd., Burslem, England, c. 1920-1964. *Courtesy of Michael L. Curtner.* $200-235.

Mark of meat dish.

Batter and syrup set with tray (batter: 8.5" h.; syrup: 6" h.; tray: 10.5" l.), Bas relief, Japan, marked "Made in Japan." Note: The pattern of the tray and syrup is unusual because it is the traditional pattern with only two people on bridge instead of three. *Courtesy of Tim & Kim Allen.* $400-500 set.

Detail of pattern on tray, showing the two people on bridge.

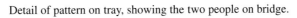

Bowls of All Sorts

Bowl, 3.25" h., 6" dia., by Henry Alcock & Co., Cobridge, England, c. 1861-1880, Godden's #64. *Courtesy of J. Dennis Crosby.* $60-75.

Punch bowl, 14.75" dia., by Villeroy & Boch, Wallerfangen, Germany, 1861-1876. Note: The break in the side of the piece was repaired with staples. *Courtesy of Joyce & Bill Keenan.* $500+ (if mint).

Detail of staples used in repair of break.

Strawberry bowl, 9.75" dia., with undertray, 10" dia., both reticulated (which provides for drainage), by W. T. Copeland, Stoke, England, 1891-1912. Rare to find set together. *Courtesy of Charles & Louise Loehr, Louise's Old Things.* $1150-1350.

Serving bowl, 2.5" h., 10" dia., with scalloped edge, Two Temples II reversed center decal in pink, USA. *Courtesy of Joyce & Bill Keenan.* $35-50.

Flat bowl, 2" h., 6.375" dia., pink willow, restaurant ware, by Jackson China Co., Falls Creek, Pennsylvania, USA, marked "Jackson China/ Cook's Hotel & Restaurant Supply Co., New York." *Courtesy of Joyce & Bill Keenan.* $40-50.

Berry bowl or dish, willow variant pattern on either side of bowl's interior, with multicolor floral center and border pattern, by Booths, Tunstall, England, marked "silicon china," c. 1906+, Godden's #453. *Courtesy of Pat & Ken Roberts.* $25-35.

Detail of pattern on saucer.

Cream soup with saucer/underplate, Pekin pattern, with ivory background, Royal Winton, by Grimwades Ltd., Stoke, England, c. 1951+, Godden's #1838. *Courtesy of Tim & Kim Allen.* $75-95.

Chapter Three
Coffee & Tea

Demitasse coffee set, including coffee pot, creamer, sugar, and five cups and saucers (set usually has six of each), Japan. *Courtesy of Joyce & Bill Keenan.* $150-200 set.

Assortment of one-cup teapots, English, American, and Japanese manufacturers. *Courtesy of Joyce & Bill Keenan.* $75-125 each.

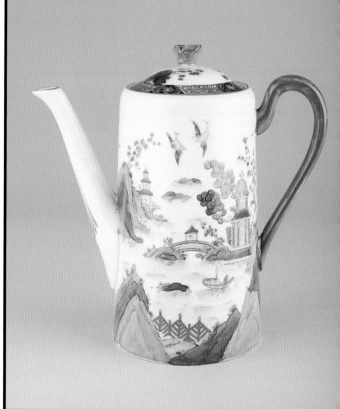

Coffee pot, 8.75" h., "Chinese Willow" pattern, by Crown Staffordshire Porcelain Co. Ltd., Fenton, England, c. 1906+, Godden's #1149. *Courtesy of Tim & Kim Allen.* $150-175.

Teapot, 8.5" h., and large sugar, 7.5" h., Two Temples II pattern with butterfly border, bow design on lids and around handle, by Ridgways, Hanley, England, c. 1878-1891. *Courtesy of Joyce & Bill Keenan.* Teapot: $260-300; sugar: $125-150.

Teapot, 6.5" h., and sugar, 5" h., Booths pattern, by Booths, Tunstall, England, c. 1912+, Godden's #454. *Courtesy of J. Dennis Crosby.* Teapot: $275-325; sugar: $125-150.

Teapot, 4.5" h., Burleigh pattern, by Burgess & Leigh, Burslem, England, c. 1930+. *Courtesy of Tim & Kim Allen.* $125-150.

Teapot, 5.5" h., with teapot trivet or stand, 5.75" dia., by Wedgwood & Co., Tunstall, England, c. 1891-1900, Godden's #4056. *Courtesy of J. Dennis Crosby.* Teapot: $250-275; stand: $100-125; $350-400 for set.

Teapot, 5.25" h., traditional pattern with dagger border on top and lid, by James Sadler & Sons, Burslem, England, c. 1947+, Godden's #3437. *Courtesy of Tim & Kim Allen.* $75-100.

Teapot, 6" h., traditional pattern with dagger border on lid, by James Sadler & Sons, Burslem, England, with raised mark of "Sadler/ England," c. 1947. *Courtesy of Tim & Kim Allen.* $60-80.

Teapot, 6 sided and footed, 6.5" h., traditional pattern with dagger border on top and lid, by James Sadler & Sons, Burslem, England, c. 1947+, Godden's #3437. *Courtesy of Tim & Kim Allen.* $150-175.

Teapot, 6.5" h. to top of handle, by James Sadler & Sons, Burslem, England, impressed "Sadler/England." *Courtesy of Tim & Kim Allen.* $75-100.

Large teapot with lid, 4" h., by Homer Laughlin China Co., East Liverpool, Ohio, USA, unmarked, c. 1900+. *Courtesy of Joyce & Bill Keenan*. $75-95.

Alternative view of teapot to show decorative handle and diamond and triangle patterned border.

Teapot, 4.25" h., Two Temples II reversed variant pattern, attributed to W. S. George Pottery Co., East Palestine, Ohio, USA, 1938. Note: Though item is unmarked, it is attributed to W. S. George Pottery Co. for its Ranchero shape, which was only made by that company in 1938. *Courtesy of Tim & Kim Allen*. $100-125.

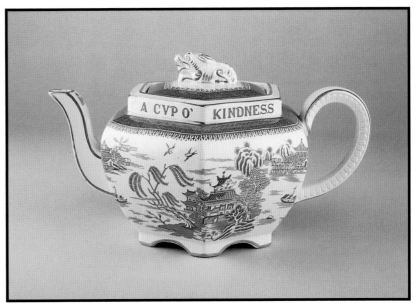

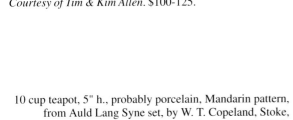

10 cup teapot, 5" h., probably porcelain, Mandarin pattern, from Auld Lang Syne set, by W. T. Copeland, Stoke, England, with British registry mark for January 7, 1879. *Courtesy of Tim & Kim Allen*. $300-350.

Teapot, 5.75" h. (to top of finial), Mandarin pattern, by Gibson & Sons, Burslem, England, c. 1950+, Godden's #1691. *Courtesy of Tim & Kim Allen.* $60-80.

Teapot with lid and wooden handle, 4.25" h. (to top of finial, not including handle), Japan. *Courtesy of Joyce & Bill Keenan.* $25-30.

Electric teapot with lid and cord (cord not shown in photo), 7.75" h., Japan. *Courtesy of Joyce & Bill Keenan.* $50-75.

Electric hot water pot with lid and cord, 5.75" h., Japan. *Courtesy of Joyce & Bill Keenan.* $50-75.

Alternate view of carafe and separate base warmer showing molded place for candle inside.

Carafe with lid, 9" h. (to top of finial), on separate base warmer, 3" h., 5" dia., Japan. *Courtesy of Joyce & Bill Keenan.* $150-175.

Mark of sugar.

Creamer and sugar with lid, both 3.25" h., by Ridgways, Hanley, England, c. 1927+. *Courtesy of Joyce & Bill Keenan.* $75-110 each.

Large creamer, 4.75" h., and sugar with lid, 4.5" h., by Charles Allerton & Sons, Longton, England, c. 1903-1912. *Courtesy of Joyce & Bill Keenan.* $125-150 each.

Mark of sugar.

Sugar with lid, 4.5" h., by Globe Pottery Co. Ltd., Cobridge, England, c. 1917+. *Courtesy of Joyce & Bill Keenan.* $45-60.

Side detail of sugar bowl.

Oval shaped sucrier or sugar bowl, no lid, 4.75" x 3", Two Temples II pattern, unmarked though attributed to John Rose & Co. (Coalport Porcelain Works), Shropshire, England, c. 1800+. *Courtesy of Joyce & Bill Keenan.* $100-125 without lid; $175-200 with lid.

Oval sugar bowl with lid, 3.5" x 2.875", by Mintons, Stoke, England, c. 1891-1901. *Courtesy of Joyce & Bill Keenan*. $75-95.

Two individual creamers. *Left:* 2" h., Two Temples II pattern, by Maddock, Burslem, England, c. 1891-1935. *Right:* 1.75" h., traditional pattern, by Shenango China Co., New Castle, Pennsylvania, USA. *Courtesy of Joyce & Bill Keenan*. $15-30 each.

Sugar and creamer, bone china, Chinese Legend pattern, by Wedgwood, England, c. 1985-1992. *Courtesy of Tim & Kim Allen*. $125-150 set.

Note: Chinese Legend pattern was a particular pattern only produced by Wedgwood for a brief time during the mid-1980s to early 1990s.

Saucer (or child's soup bowl?), 4.5" dia., with scalloped edge, England, impressed "Stevenson" on bottom, c. 1820+. *Courtesy of Joyce & Bill Keenan*. $20-25 ($60-75 if a soup bowl).

Demitasse cup and saucer, Turner center pattern with scroll and flower border, by Mason's, England, c. 1891+. *Courtesy of Joyce & Bill Keenan.* $40-60.

Large cup and saucer, Burleigh Ware, by Burgess & Leigh, Burslem, England, c. 1930s. *Courtesy of Joyce & Bill Keenan.* $15-25.

Cup and saucer, bone china, by A. B. Jones & Sons, Longton, England, c. 1949+. *Courtesy of Joyce & Bill Keenan.* $25-30.

Teacup, from Auld Lang Syne set, England. *Courtesy of Tim & Kim Allen.* $65-95.

Mark of saucer.

Saucer, 6" dia., with scalloped edge, by Buffalo Pottery Co., Buffalo, New York, USA, c. 1904+. *Courtesy of Joyce & Bill Keenan.* $10-15.

Demitasse cup and saucer, by Booths, Tunstall, England, c. 1906+. *Courtesy of Tim & Kim Allen.* $35-50.

Teacup and saucer, pink willow, by Alfred Meakin, Tunstall, England, c. 1930+. *Courtesy of Joyce & Bill Keenan.* $15-18.

Mark of saucer.

Trio (teacup, saucer, and dessert plate), porcelain, multicolor pictorial border showing elements of willow pattern, marked "ECCH/Made in England." *Courtesy of Tim & Kim Allen.* $40-60 set.

Teacup and saucer, porcelain, with lithopane (Geisha girl on bottom), multicolor decal, Japan, modern. *Courtesy of Tim & Kim Allen.* $15-20.

Teacup and saucer, porcelain, hand painted with gold detailing, Japan. *Courtesy of Tim & Kim Allen.* $35-45.

Mark of saucer.

Demitasse cup and saucer, blue border containing pictorial willow pattern in gold, trimmed with 22kt gold, by Pacific China, USA, c. 1937+. *Courtesy of Joyce & Bill Keenan.* $35-45.

Tea set, part of service for six, including cake plate, creamer, open sugar, cup, saucer, and dessert plates, porcelain, by A. B. Jones & Sons, Longton, England, c. 1930+, Godden's #2197. *Courtesy of Tim & Kim Allen.* $275-325 for grouping.

Tea set (including teapot, cup & saucer, creamer, sugar, and plate), porcelain, green with willow pattern in gold and enamel decaling, marked "Hand painted/Made in Japan" and showing two T's with interlocking diamonds. *Courtesy of Tim & Kim Allen.* $350-375 for grouping.

Teapot, 5" h., with creamer and sugar, both 3" h., Mandarin pattern on black background, by Gibson & Sons, Burslem, England, c. 1950+, Godden's #1691. *Courtesy of Tim & Kim Allen.* Teapot: $175-200; creamer/sugar: $75-100 pair.

Teapot, 5" h., with creamer and sugar, both 3" h., chrome, known as "Willo-Ware" pattern by manufacturer, by Swan Brand, England, marked "Swan-Cromalin," c. 1970s. *Courtesy of Tim & Kim Allen.* $150-175 for set.

Two cups, 2.75" h., and saucers, 5" dia., blue willow center pattern with daisy border in red, by William Alsager Adderley, Longton, England, impressed "W. A. A. Ivory," 1876-1885. *Courtesy of Tom & Barbara Allen.* $100-125 (for single cup/saucer set).

Teapot, 6.75" h., creamer, 3.25" h., and sugar, 5" h., also showing blue willow center pattern with daisy border in red, unmarked, however part of set with cups and saucers, by William Alsager Adderley, Longton, England, 1876-1885. *Courtesy of Tom & Barbara Allen.* $350-400 for grouping (teapot, creamer, and sugar).

Mark of tea keeper.

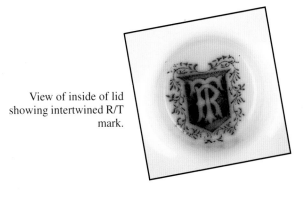

View of inside of lid showing intertwined R/T mark.

Tea keeper with lid, 8" h., England, marked on bottom "Ringtons Limited./Tea Merchants./Newcastle upon Tyne.," c. 1859-1890. *Courtesy of Joyce & Bill Keenan.* $350-400.

Tea keeper, no lid, 6.75" h., Two Temples II pattern with butterfly border, marked on bottom "Thomas & Evans/Celebrated Tevna Tea," date unknown. *Courtesy of Joyce & Bill Keenan.* $150-175 without lid (if mint).

Detail of bottom of tea keeper (*right*).

Detail of top of tin.

"Tea" tin, 5.5" h., England. *Courtesy of Tim & Kim Allen*. $125-150.

Four "Tea" canisters, 4.5" average height, chrome, showing different variations of willow pattern, etched or raised, England. Each have different finials. *Courtesy of Tim & Kim Allen*. $50-75 each.

Close-up of one of the canisters from set.

Close-up of another canister from set.

Chapter Four
Pitchers & Jugs

Two pitchers. *Left:* 3.75" h., England, c. 1891+. *Right:* 4.5" h., by Thomas Forester & Sons Ltd., Longton, England, marked "Phoenix Ware," c. 1891+. *Courtesy of Joyce & Bill Keenan.* $40-50 each.

From left to right: Pitcher, 7.375" h., gold gilding on handle and lip edge, Coronaware, by Sampson Hancock & Sons, Stoke, England, c. 1912-1937, Godden's #1935; milk jug, 6.25" h., England, c. pre-1891; pitcher, 6.375" h., marked "Warranted/Staffordshire/W.A. & Co. T./England," c. 1893-1917. *Courtesy of Joyce & Bill Keenan.* $110-135 each.

Mark of milk pitcher.

Milk pitcher, 5.25" h., Burleigh Ware, by Burgess & Leigh, Burslem, England, c. 1930+, Godden's #723 with "Made in England." *Courtesy of Tim & Kim Allen.* $35-45.

Syrup pitcher, 3.75" h., flow blue, traditional pattern, by Doulton & Co., Burslem, England, c. 1891-1902. (Usually these had a pewter lid.) *Courtesy of Joyce & Bill Keenan.* $260-295 with lid.

Milk pitcher, 4" h., by James Sadler & Sons, Burslem, England, 1947+, Godden's #3437. *Courtesy of Tim & Kim Allen.* $50-75.

Milk jug (*left*), 4.75" h., silver lustre, hand painted variant pattern, Lancaster & Sandland Ltd., Hanley, England, 1949+, Godden's #2328, (with small creamer, 2.5" h., copper lustre, by Lancaster & Sandland Ltd., Hanley, England, 1949+, Godden's #2327). *Courtesy of Tim & Kim Allen.* $40-60 each.

Detail of top border.

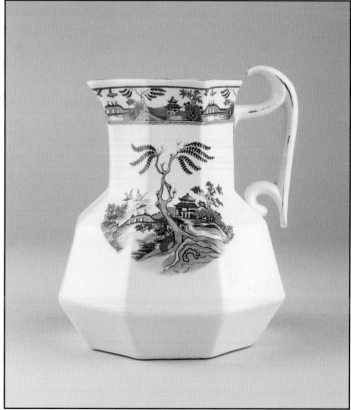

Pitcher, 7" h., highly unusual, multicolor decal with pictorial border at top, Booths pattern, by Booths, Tunstall, England, c. 1906+, similar to Godden's #453 with "Silicone China" in ribbon. *Courtesy of Tim & Kim Allen.* $250-275.

Hot water pitcher, 5.25" h. (to top of lip), clobbered, by Josiah Wedgwood & Sons, Burslem, England, June 1913, impressed "Wedgwood" and "3TP." *Courtesy of Tim & Kim Allen.* $200-235.

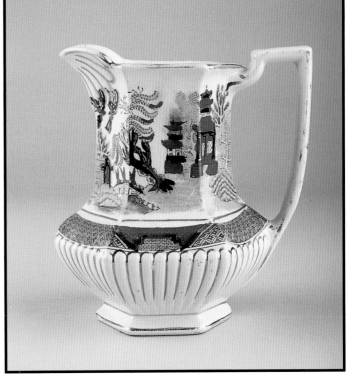

Pitcher, 6" h., clobbered with gold detailing, by Gater, Hall & Co., Tunstall, England, c. 1914+, Godden's #1672. *Courtesy of Tim & Kim Allen.* $200-235.

Pitcher, 7.25" h. (to top of lip), enamel, hand painted on gold transfer print, by S. Fielding & Co., Stoke, England, c. 1930, Godden's #1551 and impressed "E20." *Courtesy of Tim & Kim Allen.* $275-300.

Pitcher, 4.25" h., Basaltine willow, by Frank Beardmore & Co., Fenton, England, c. 1903-1914, Godden's #307a. *Courtesy of Tim & Kim Allen.* $275-300.

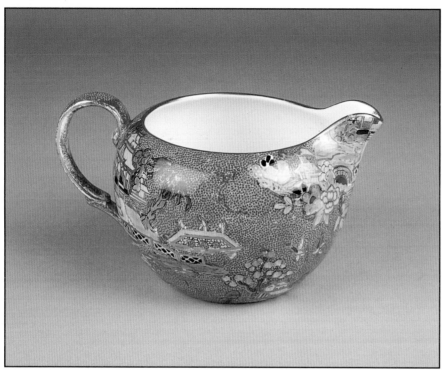

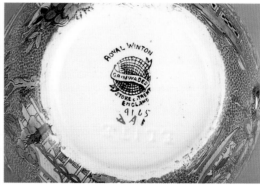

Mark of jug with Elite shape name impressed on bottom.

Small pitcher or jug, 3.5" h., Elite shape (shape name impressed on bottom), Pekin pattern, with stippled purplish-red background, Royal Winton, by Grimwades Ltd., Stoke, England, c. 1930s. *Courtesy of Tom & Barbara Allen.* $175-200.

Chicago jug, 4" h., by Buffalo Pottery Co., Buffalo, New York, USA, 1906. *Courtesy of Tim & Kim Allen.* $300-350.

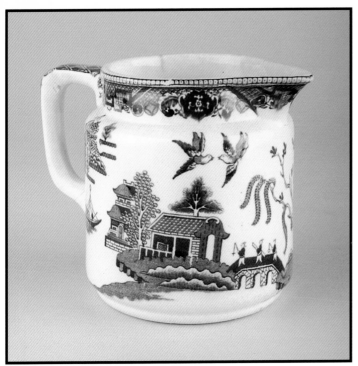

Pitcher, no lid, 4.5" h., by Buffalo Pottery Co., Buffalo, New York, USA, 1910. *Courtesy of Joyce & Bill Keenan.* $275-295 with lid.

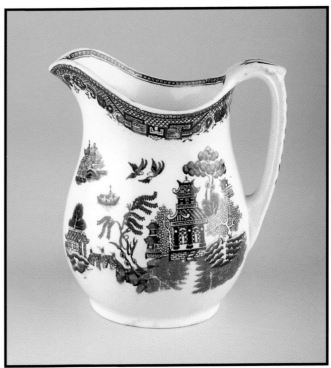

Pitcher, 6" h., made for distributor L. Straus & Sons in New York, England. *Courtesy of Joyce & Bill Keenan.* $60-75.

Mark of pitcher.

Pitcher, 4" h., by Buffalo Pottery Co., Buffalo, New York, USA, 1911. *Courtesy of Joyce & Bill Keenan.* $135-150.

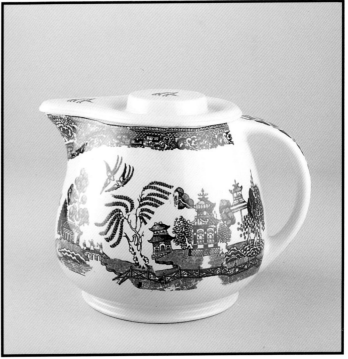

Covered jug, 6" h., unusual, blue traditional transfer print on Fiesta shape, by Homer Laughlin China Co., East Liverpool, Ohio, USA, c. 1937-1938. *Courtesy of Tim & Kim Allen.* $125-150.

Milk pitcher, 5.25" h., Japan. *Courtesy of Joyce & Bill Keenan.* $75-95.

One-pint milk bottle or jug, 7" h., decal underglaze, unmarked though probably USA. *Courtesy of Joyce & Bill Keenan.* $15-20.

Pitcher, 8.5" h., with set of four tumblers, 3.5" h., Japan, un-marked. Note the pattern of one tumbler (*second from right*) appears slightly blurred in comparison to others. *Courtesy of Joyce & Bill Keenan.* Pitcher: $125-150; tumblers: $20-25 each; $250-275 for set.

Chapter Five
Condiment Pieces

Salt and pepper shakers, 3" h., unusual, traditional transfer print on Fiesta shape, by Homer Laughlin China Co., East Liverpool, Ohio, USA, c. 1937-1938. *Courtesy of Tim & Kim Allen.* $50-60 pair.

Salt and pepper shakers, 2.5" h., Japan. *Courtesy of Joyce & Bill Keenan.* $15-18 pair.

Teapot shaped salt and pepper shakers, 3" h., unmarked, but of Japanese origin. *Courtesy of Joyce & Bill Keenan.* $35-45 pair.

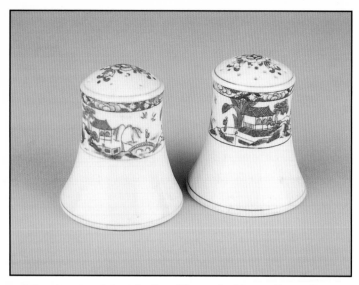

Salt and pepper shakers, by Royal Sometuke, Nippon, Japan. *Courtesy of Joyce & Bill Keenan.* $20-25 pair.

Salt and pepper shakers, 4.5" h., unusual, hand carved ivory-like material, willow variant pattern, unknown origin. *Courtesy of Pat & Ken Roberts.* $125-140 pair.

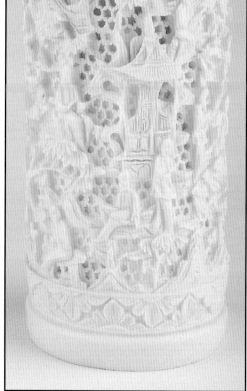

Detail of carved handiwork.

Sugar shaker with metal top, 6" h., multicolor variant pattern, by Lancaster & Sons, Hanley, England, c. 1938-1944. *Courtesy of Joyce & Bill Keenan.* $160-195.

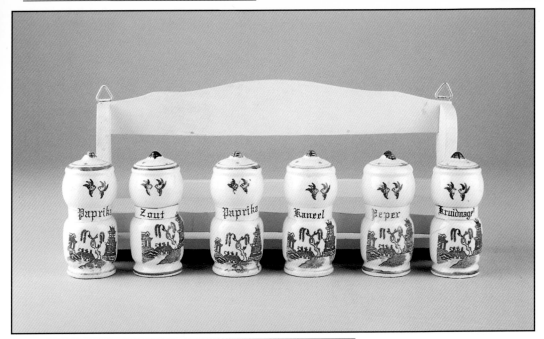

Set of spice shakers, 3" h. each, spice names applied with decals, appear to be of Japanese manufacture, c. 1950s. Note the spice names are in German. *Courtesy of Tim & Kim Allen.* $225-275.

Saltbox with wooden lid, 5" x 4.75" x 3.5", Japan. *Courtesy of Joyce & Bill Keenan.* $200-275.

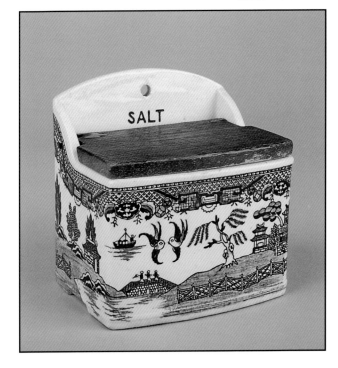

Tea-light holder or candle holder (to be placed under butter stand to keep butter warm), 1.25" h., willow border pattern, Japan. *Courtesy of J. Dennis Crosby.* $10-15.

Assortment of footed salt dips, 0.75" h., 1.5" dia., porcelain, turned to show various scenes from willow pattern, by Royal Sometuke, Nippon, Japan, c. 1906. *Courtesy of Tim & Kim Allen.* $25-30 each.

Selection of assorted butter pats: English, American, and Japanese manufacturers. *Courtesy of Joyce & Bill Keenan.* $15-40 (depending on manufacturer).

Butter dish with wooden holder, 4" dia., England. *Courtesy of Joyce & Bill Keenan.* $75-95.

Relish dish, 5.375" dia., with scalloped edge, England, marked "Stoneware." *Courtesy of Joyce & Bill Keenan.* $75-100.

Mustard jar with lid, 2.625" h., 2.5" dia., by John Maddock & Sons, Burslem, England, c. 1896-1906. *Courtesy of Joyce & Bill Keenan.* $25-35.

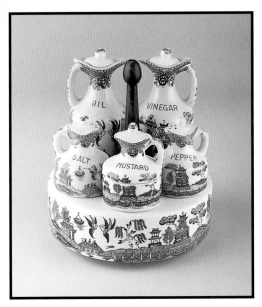

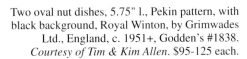

Castor condiment (or lazy susan) set on revolving stand, usually with mustard spoon, marked "Made in Japan," c. 1940s-1950s. *Courtesy of Tim & Kim Allen.* $140-200 (if complete).

Two oval nut dishes, 5.75" l., Pekin pattern, with black background, Royal Winton, by Grimwades Ltd., England, c. 1951+, Godden's #1838. *Courtesy of Tim & Kim Allen.* $95-125 each.

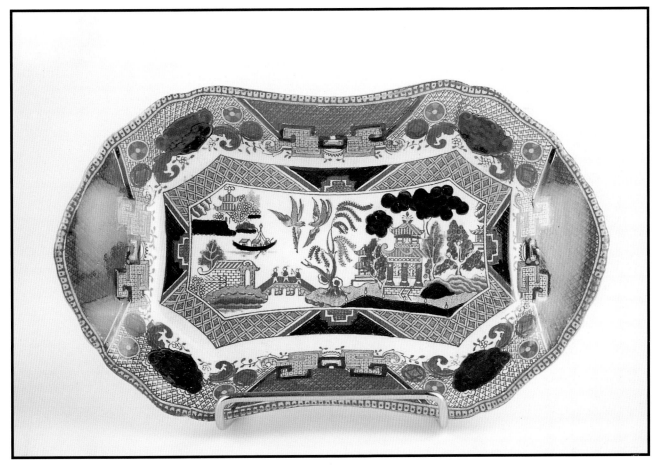

Pickle dish, 4.5" x 8", Gaudy Willow, by Buffalo Pottery Co., Buffalo, New York, USA, 1908. *Courtesy of Tim & Kim Allen.* $250-300.

Chapter Six
Bed, Bath & More

Ginger jar with lid, 4.75" h., by James Sadler & Sons, Burslem, England, raised mark on bottom, c. 1937+. *Courtesy of Joyce & Bill Keenan.* $25-35.

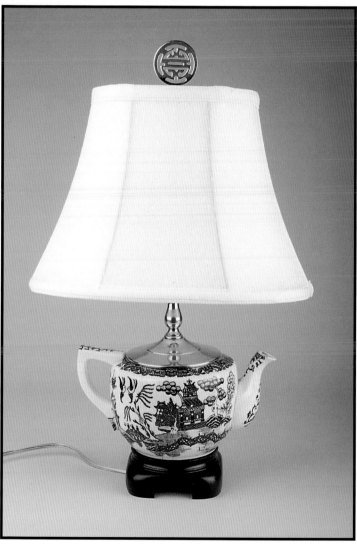

Lamp made from willow ware teapot, mounted on wooden base and electrified. Teapot is of Japanese manufacturer. *Courtesy of Joyce & Bill Keenan.* $125-145.

Ginger jar with lid, 4" h., 4" dia., pink willow, Turner pattern, by Mason's, England, c. 1891+, Godden's #143-5. *Courtesy of Joyce & Bill Keenan.* $35-45.

Pin dish, 3" sq., by Booths, Tunstall, England, marked "Real Old Willow," c. 1905. *Courtesy of Pat & Ken Roberts.* $40-55.

Dresser set (including dresser tray, 13.5" x 8.5", powder box, 4.5" dia., two small trinket boxes, 3.5" dia., and one large trinket box, 4" dia.), multicolor decal, by Thomas Lawrence Ltd., Longton, England, marked "Falcon Ware" by manufacturer, c. 1936+, Godden's #2342. *Courtesy of Tim & Kim Allen.* $375-450 for set.

Rose bowl, 8 sided, very unusual, bright blue matte body with hand painted multicolor enameled over gold transfer, by John Tams Ltd., England, c. 1912+, Godden's #3793 with "John Tams Ltd./Stoke-on-Trent/England." *Courtesy of Tim & Kim Allen.* $425-450.

Pair of candlesticks, 6.25" h., positioned to show various scenes from willow pattern, by John Tams Ltd., England, c. 1912+. *Courtesy of Tom & Barbara Allen.* $450-475 pair.

Vase, 5.25" h., Staffa shape (shape name impressed on bottom), Pekin pattern, with turquoise background, Royal Winton, by Grimwades Ltd., Stoke, England, c. 1934-1950, Godden's #1835. *Courtesy of Tom & Barbara Allen.* $225-250.

Vase with flare top, 7.25" h., bone china, Chinese Legend pattern, by Wedgwood, England, marked "Wedgwood, bone china, made in England," c. 1985-1992. *Courtesy of Tim & Kim Allen.* $125-150.

Close-up showing Staffa shape name impressed on bottom.

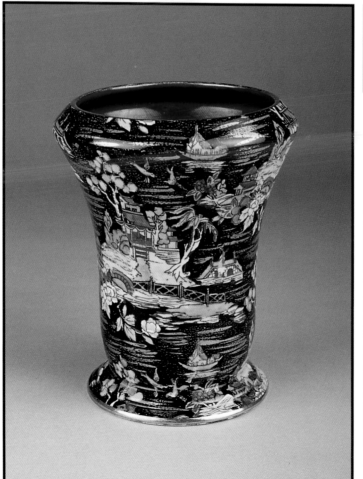

Vase, 6" h., Pekin pattern, with black background and red interior, Royal Winton, by Grimwades Ltd., Stoke, England, c. 1934-1950. *Courtesy of Tom & Barbara Allen.* $200-225.

Mark of vase.

Leaf dish, 9" l., enamel, hand painted on gold transfer print, by S. Fielding & Co., Stoke, England, c. 1930, Godden's #1551 and impressed "E20." *Courtesy of Tim & Kim Allen.* $275-300.

Two dresser boxes, 1.5" x 5", Pekin pattern, left with blue background and right with green background, Royal Winton, by Grimwades Ltd., Stoke, England, marked "J-W.Co. Staffordshire England Royal Winton." c. 1930+. *Courtesy of Tim & Kim Allen.* $150-175 each.

Dresser box, 2" x 4.25", Pekin pattern, with stipple blue background, Royal Winton, by Grimwades Ltd., Stoke, England, marked "J-W.Co. Staffordshire England." c. 1930+. *Courtesy of Tim & Kim Allen.* $175-200.

Close-up of top of dresser box.

From left: Chamber pot, 5.25" h., 9" dia., and wash pitcher (or ewer), 10.25" h., with wash basin, 4.5" h., 15.125" dia., England. *Courtesy of Joyce & Bill Keenan.* $700-850 for 3 piece set.

Wash basin, 5" h., 16" dia., clobbered, by Josiah Wedgwood, England, impressed "Wedgwood" and "3NO," November 1912. (Note the appearance of the traditional pattern on inside and Two Temples II on the outside; unusual to show both patterns.) *Courtesy of Tim & Kim Allen.*

Ewer, 9" h. to lip (11.25" h. to top of handle), clobbered, by Josiah Wedgwood, England, impressed "Wedgwood" and "3NO," November 1912. *Courtesy of Tim & Kim Allen.* $800-1200 for 2 piece set of clobbered ewer and wash basin.

Alternative view of wash basin showing Two Temples II pattern on outside.

Ewer, 9.25" h., and wash basin, 4.25" h., 16" dia., multicolor reverse traditional decal. *Courtesy of Tim & Kim Allen.* $400-500.

Ewer, 12" h., and wash basin, 5" h., 15.5" dia., bright blue matte body with hand painted multicolor enameled over gold transfer, Tams Ware, by John Tams Ltd., Longton, England, c. 1912+, Godden's #3793 with "John Tams Ltd./Stoke-on-Trent/England." *Courtesy of Tim & Kim Allen.* $700-850.

Chamber pot, part of Tams Ware wash set, 5.75" h., 9.25" dia. *Courtesy of Tim & Kim Allen.* $350-375.

From left: Toothbrush holder, 6" h., and soap dish, 3.5" h., 5.125" dia., part of Tams Ware wash set. *Courtesy of Tim & Kim Allen.* Toothbrush holder: $250-275; soap dish: $250-275.

Chamber pot with lid, 5.25" h., 9.5" dia., England. *Courtesy of Pat & Ken Roberts.* $250-300 (lid adds value).

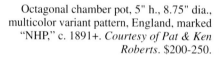

Octagonal chamber pot, 5" h., 8.75" dia., multicolor variant pattern, England, marked "NHP," c. 1891+. *Courtesy of Pat & Ken Roberts.* $200-250.

Ceramic wall tile, 6" sq., unmarked though attributed to Minton, Stoke, England. *Courtesy of J. Dennis Crosby.* $75-95.

Square tile or trivet, 6" sq., by Soriano Ceramics. *Courtesy of Joyce & Bill Keenan.* $40-50.

Round trivet in wooden base, 7.5" dia., marked "Made in Philippines" (though center tile probably made in England). *Courtesy of Joyce & Bill Keenan*. $20-30.

Square trivet with woven cane around edges, 6" sq., England. *Courtesy of Joyce & Bill Keenan*. $95-125.

Butter trivet/drainer, 4" dia., showing elements of traditional willow pattern, England. *Courtesy of Joyce & Bill Keenan*. $75-100.

Two tin burner covers (sold in sets of four with 2 of each size). *Courtesy of Joyce & Bill Keenan*. $8-10 for set of four.

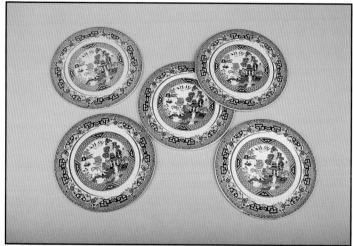

Assortment of hot plates, by Nesco-Metal-Besco. *Courtesy of Joyce & Bill Keenan*. $5-8 each.

Biscuit jar with sterling silver lid, 5" h., attributed to W. T. Copeland, Stoke, England, c. mid- to late-1800s. *Courtesy of Joyce & Bill Keenan*. 250-325.

Wine coaster, 1" h., 4.25" dia., Parrott pattern, Royal Winton, by Grimwades Ltd., Stoke, England, c. 1930+. *Courtesy of Tim & Kim Allen.* $60-75.

Ash tray, 3.625" dia., possibly of Japanese manufacturer. *Courtesy of Joyce & Bill Keenan.* $10-12.

Lighter in shape of teacup, with saucer, Japan, c. 1950s. *Courtesy of Tim & Kim Allen.* $125-150. Note: Also commands value as a novelty item.

Chapter Seven
Miscellany

Early summer of 1999 I had the pleasure of attending the annual convention of the IWC, held that year in Richmond, Virginia. Here, during the dealer sale, I noticed what I thought of as a rather unusual and interesting piece. It was an old wooden crate that I can only assume was once used for the storage of pieces of willow from the kiln or used in the transport of the wares from the factory to the distributor. The owner of the crate had it adapted for use as a table, which resembled a sort of chopping block form, with four peg-like legs, the crate on top, and a hinged lid that latched closed. The words "Willow Ware," original to the crate, appeared stenciled on the crate's sides in black lettering. How very functional and ingenious I thought—what a unique piece for a collector of willow ware.

I had discovered what some of you may already know or what others of you may soon embark upon: willow ware really does come in all forms. And, just when you think you've seen it all—look again, there's more: jewelry boxes with drawers lined with willow-patterned cloth, teddy bears dressed in willow-patterned attire, candles with the willow pattern, clothing, jewelry, lamps, and much more. Many collectors love and enjoy their willow so much that they want nothing else than to surround themselves with it. Like the willow crate that had been adapted for use as a table, willow teapots are made into functional lamps and shards of broken plates customized to form earrings, brooches, or even hairclips. Some put their artistic talents to use by hand painting willow designs onto pieces of furniture or stenciling willow designs on the walls of a room in their home. Look for some of these unique, personalized examples of willow throughout. They may give you some innovative ideas your own, and allow you to adapt pieces of your collection for maximum use and display.

Paper Products

Postcard, c. 1960, with "Legend of the Chinese willow ware" printed on front. Carmen and Casey and Distributed exclusively by Copyright Owners, Box 10044 Main Station, St. Petersburg 33, Florida, USA. Back reads: "According to an old Chinese legend, the pretty daughter of a Chinese Mandarin refused to marry a wealthy, old suitor favored by her father. She eloped with her father's secretary." *Courtesy of Tim & Kim Allen*. $1-2 (new).

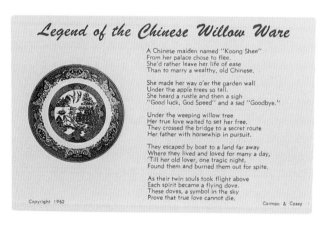

Notecard with willow pattern and "The Blue Willow Legend" printed on back, from The Blue Willow Bed & Breakfast, Seattle, WA. *Courtesy of Tim & Kim Allen*. $1-2 (new).

Greeting card picturing willow tea set on front (tray, teapot, pitcher, and two cups and saucers). Printed by Creative Papers, by C.R. Gibson. *Courtesy of Tim & Kim Allen*. $1-2 (new).

Greeting card with slot for tea bag. Inserted in slot is a Fortunes Green Tea bag, not original to card. Tea bag also has willow pattern on it. Card printed by New Harmony Greeting Cups Company, Philadelphia, Pennsylvania, USA. *Courtesy of Tim & Kim Allen.* $4-5 (new).

Three gift tags, each showing teacup with willow pattern. *Courtesy of Tim & Kim Allen.* $1-2 each (new).

Left: Greeting card showing kitten drinking from a willow cup and saucer. Printed in Pleasant Hill, California, USA. *Right*: Greeting card in shape of similar image of kitten drinking from willow cup and saucer. Printed by The Gifted Line, John Grossman, Inc. *Courtesy of Tim & Kim Allen.* $1-2 (new).

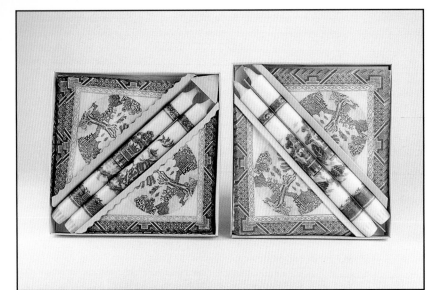

Old Willow 2 Candles and 20 Napkins, Aladdin, made in Denmark. Shown in blue and pink. *Courtesy of Tim & Kim Allen.* $30-50 for either set.

Cover of box for blue Old Willow candles and napkins.

Tea box, Fortunes Green Tea, wood, 5.25" h. *Courtesy of Joyce & Bill Keenan.* $5-6.

Fabrics

Linen tablecloth. *Courtesy of Joyce & Bill Keenan.* $45-65.

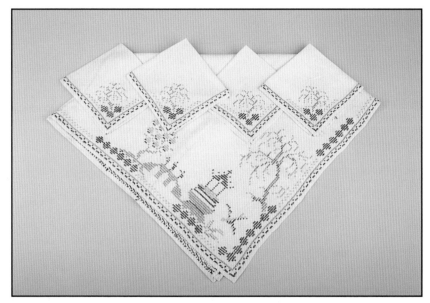

Cross-stitched bridge set showing willow pattern. *Courtesy of Joyce & Bill Keenan.* $45-65 for set.

Two sets of 'matkins,' showing willow pattern in blue and red, by Symtex. *Courtesy of Joyce & Bill Keenan.* $4-5 each.

Linen runner, 31" x 17", showing willow pattern. *Courtesy of Joyce & Bill Keenan.* $12-18.

Two placemats, by Johnson Bros. Ltd., contemporary. *Courtesy of Joyce & Bill Keenan.* $5-6 each.

Tablecloth, by Johnson Bros. Ltd., contemporary. *Courtesy of Joyce & Bill Keenan.* $35-45.

Canvas tote bag showing depiction of willow pattern. *Courtesy of Joyce & Bill Keenan.* $8-12.

Jewelry & Accessories

Some collectibles are fashioned by hand and homemade. Pricing these items is difficult because of their uniqueness and one-of-a-kind nature—willow jewelry is one good example, and as such, jewelry items remain unpriced (along with a few other hard-to-price willow collectibles).

Pair of earrings made from Burleigh Ware shards. *Courtesy of Joyce & Bill Keenan.*

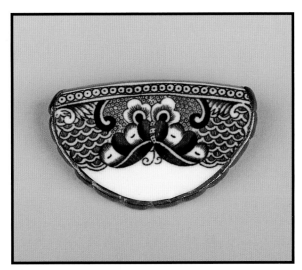

Brooch made from Burleigh Ware shards. *Courtesy of Joyce & Bill Keenan.*

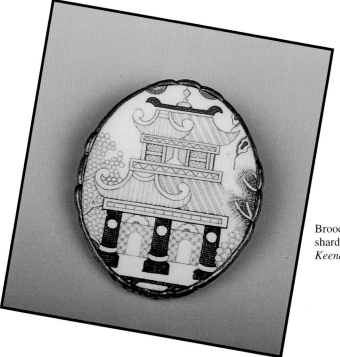

Brooch made from willow ware shards. *Courtesy of Joyce & Bill Keenan.*

Lady's compact, 3.25" dia., unmarked though attributed to English manufacturer, c. 1930s. *Courtesy of Charles & Louise Loehr, Louise's Old Things.* $195-275 (rare).

Jewelry box, 12.5" x 8" x 5.5", possibly rosewood with jade inlay, red brass metal work, and top handle. Drawers are lined with red satin brocade embroidered with willow variant pattern. Age unknown. *Courtesy of Shirley & James Hillier.* $150-200.

Detail of red satin brocade showing embroidered willow pattern.

Boxes & Tins

Charming, relatively inexpensive, offered in a variety of shapes, sizes, colors, materials, and patterns, willow boxes and tins earn appeal with collectors, as they are suitable for any corner of a room, offer smaller, functional examples of the items decorated in the willow pattern, and add variety and assortment to any medley of willow collectibles. A May 1999 article from *The Willow Review* offers up the following information and valuing tips for collectors of willow boxes and tins. They can be found in a range of prices, from one dollar to upwards of one hundred dollars, depending on age and condition; those made from tin or metal that remain in excellent condition are considered very desirable, as these materials tend to be very susceptible to rusting and fading (especially if previously exposed to sunlight). For older boxes and tins, look for differences in the color on the sides and top; this will be an indication of fading and can give you a better idea of the item's condition and worth. (However, very rare items may still command high prices despite not being in the best of condition. And beware, just because an item shows signs of rust or fading does not necessarily mean it is old.) Boxes and tins also find appeal as they turn up in places other than those specifically known to deal in the willow pattern: yard sales and flea markets offer just such opportunities (not to mention the other willow bargains that may be had there). Be on the lookout for the older, more unusual containers. These were originally produced to hold candy or food and were not bought with the intention of being preserved or even kept.

Some manufacturers today are still making containers decorated in the willow pattern; a trip to your local food store may yield a few examples. If not, some contemporary willow-patterned tins and boxes are shown here, along with a few choice older items. Take special notice of the willow tin in pink. Curiously enough, the figures on the bridge are all clearly women!

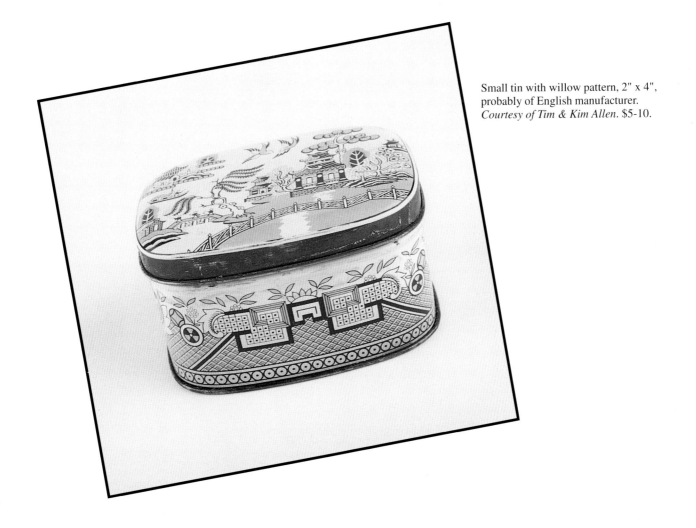

Small tin with willow pattern, 2" x 4", probably of English manufacturer. *Courtesy of Tim & Kim Allen.* $5-10.

Large tin with willow pattern (floral pattern around sides), 2" x 8", probably of English manufacturer. *Courtesy of Tim & Kim Allen.* $5-10.

Left: Tin with willow pattern and sleeping cat on top, 2" h. $5-10. *Right:* Tin for English Breakfast tea with teapot, teacup, and saucer in willow pattern on front, 3.5" h. $3-5. *Courtesy of Joyce & Bill Keenan.*

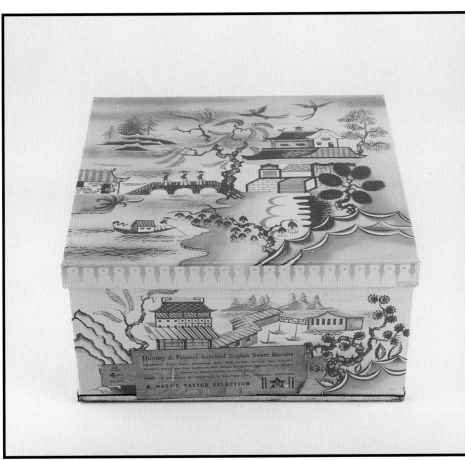

Tin for Huntley & Palmers Assorted English Sweet Biscuits, showing willow pattern in pink, 5" h. x 9.25" l., made in Reading, England. Note the figures on the bridge are clearly women. *Courtesy of Tim & Kim Allen.* $75-95.

Close-up showing women on bridge.

Metal candy tin with hinged lid, 3.5" h., white background with multicolor willow variant pattern, made in England for a company located in Long Island, New York. *Courtesy of Joyce & Bill Keenan.* $25-50.

Wooden hinged box, 2" h. x 4" l. x 3.5" w., black background with multicolor willow variant pattern, marked "Made in Great Britain." *Courtesy of Pat & Ken Roberts.* $95-125.

Round, hand painted box to hold supper tray, 10.25" dia., black background with multicolor willow variant pattern. *Courtesy of Joyce & Bill Keenan.* $75-100.

Assortment of metal candy tins, ranging in size from 2" to 5.75", dark blue background with multicolor willow variant pattern. *Courtesy of Joyce & Bill Keenan.* $15-35 (depending on manufacturer and size).

Whimsy

Bell, 4" h., bone china, "Chinese Willow" pattern, by Coalport Porcelain Works, Shropshire, England, c. 1960+, Godden's #962. *Courtesy of Tim & Kim Allen.* $15-20.

Assortment of thimbles, 0.75" to 1.25" h. *From far left to right:* Royal Crown Derby, Gimbel and Sons, Japan, and two thought to be of English manufacturer. *Courtesy of Tim & Kim Allen.* $5-15 (depending on manufacturer).

Teapot in shape of Christmas tree, decorated with miniature cups and saucers in willow pattern; base also repeats willow pattern. *Courtesy of Joyce & Bill Keenan.* $50-75.

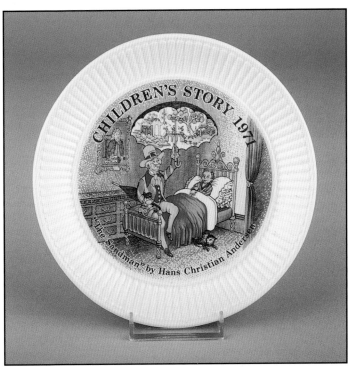

Plate, 6" dia., from "Children's Stories," a series for young collectors, 1971 edition, illustrating a scene from Hans Christian Anderson's *The Sandman*, willow pattern shown in umbrella, by Wedgwood, England. *Courtesy of Tim & Kim Allen.* $85-110.

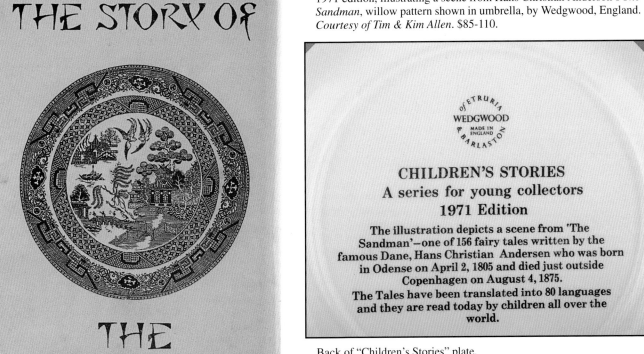

FOURTH PRINTING

THE STORY OF

THE WILLOW PATTERN PLATE

OF ETRURIA
WEDGWOOD
MADE IN
ENGLAND
& BARLASTON

CHILDREN'S STORIES
A series for young collectors
1971 Edition

The illustration depicts a scene from 'The Sandman'—one of 156 fairy tales written by the famous Dane, Hans Christian Andersen who was born in Odense on April 2, 1805 and died just outside Copenhagen on August 4, 1875.
The Tales have been translated into 80 languages and they are read today by children all over the world.

Back of "Children's Stories" plate.

Book, *The Story of the Willow Pattern Plate*, John Baker Publishers, London, England, 1970. *Courtesy of Tim & Kim Allen.* $5-10.

Child's dinner set (not complete set), including two covered vegetables, two sizes of platters, three sizes of plates, soup tureen, and gravy boat, Bridgeless pattern, attributed to Davenport, Longport, England, c. 1810. *Courtesy of Charles & Louise Loehr, Louise's Old Things*. $1000-1350 for grouping.

Child's grill plate, 4.313" dia., Japan, new. *Courtesy of Joyce & Bill Keenan*. $10-15 (if marked "Japan": $60-75).

Hand made teddy bear, 11.5" tall, made of synthetic mohair, fully jointed, with glass eyes and music box inside. Pads and vest are hand painted with willow pattern. *Courtesy of Keith A. Brower*.

Bibliography

Allen, Tim. *Handout,* entitled "Willow Pattern China. A brief study of the Willow Pattern: Its variations and history." Unpublished, 1990s.

Altman, Seymour and Violet. *The Book of Buffalo Pottery.* West Chester, Pennsylvania: Schiffer Publishing Ltd., 1969.

Bockol, Leslie. *Willow Ware: Ceramics in the Chinese Tradition.* Atglen, Pennsylvania: Schiffer Publishing Ltd., 1995.

Brenner, Robert. *Depression Glass for Collectors.* Atglen, Pennsylvania: Schiffer Publishing Ltd., 1998.

Brooke, Bob. "Diversity makes blue and white ware fun." *Antique Week,* Monday, 31 May 1999 (Vol. 32, No. 11), sec. 1, p. 1, 14, 36.

Camehl, Ada Walker. *The Blue-China Book.* E.P. Dutton & Company, (Halcyon House edition, published and distributed by Blue Ribbon Books, Inc., New York) 1916.

Coysh, A.W., and R.K. Henrywood. *The Dictionary of Blue and White Printed Pottery 1780-1880,* vol. 1. Suffolk, United Kingdom: Antique Collectors' Club Ltd., 1982.

Cunningham, Jo. *Homer Laughlin: A Giant Among Dishes 1873-1939.* Atglen, Pennsylvania: Schiffer Publishing Ltd., 1998.

_____. *The Best of Collectible Dinnerware.* Rev. 2nd ed. Atglen, Pennsylvania: Schiffer Publishing Ltd., 1999.

Gaston, Mary Frank. *Blue Willow.* Rev. 2nd ed. Paducah, Kentucky: Collector Books, 1990.

Godden, Geoffery A., F.R.S.A. *An Illustrated Encyclopedia of British Pottery and Porcelain.* New York: Crown Publishers Inc., 1966.

_____. *British Porcelain: An Illustrated Guide.* New York: Clarkson N. Potter, Inc./Publisher, 1974; distributed by Crown Publishers, Inc.

_____. *Caughley and Worcester Porcelains 1775-1800.* New York: Frederick A. Praeger, *Publishers,* 1969.

_____. *Encyclopaedia of British Pottery and Porcelain Marks.* Exton, Pennsylvania: Schiffer Publishing Ltd., 1964.

Hughes, Bernard and Therle. *The Collector's Encyclopaedia of English Ceramics.* London: Abbey Library, 1968.

Hume, Ivor Noël. *A Guide to Artifacts of Colonial America.* New York: Alfred A. Knopf, 1985.

International Willow Collectors' Annual Convention Catalogs. 1994-1998.

Kovel, Ralph & Terry. *Kovels' New Dictionary of Marks.* New York: Crown Publishers, Inc., 1986.

Kowalsky, Arnold A., and Dorothy E. Kolwasky. *Encyclopedia of Marks 1780-1980.* Atglen, Pennsylvania: Schiffer Publishing Ltd., 1999.

Maust, Don A., ed. *Collectable Chinese Art and Antiques.* 1st ed. Uniontown, Pennsylvania: E.G. Warman Publishing, Inc., 1973.

Quintner, David Richard. *Willow!* Ontario: General Store Publishing House, 1997.

Roberts, Gaye Blake, ed. *True Blue: Transfer Printed Earthenware.* Oxfordshire: Friends of Blue, 1998.

Siptak, Jeff W. "Willow Boxes." *The Willow Review* 1, no. 2 (May 1999): 1, 3.

Snyder, Jeffrey B. *A Pocket Guide to Flow Blue.* Atglen, Pennsylvania: Schiffer Publishing Ltd., 1995.

_____. *Fiesta.* Rev. & exp. 2nd ed. Atglen, Pennsylvania: Schiffer Publishing Ltd., 1999.

_____. *Flow Blue: A Collector's Guide to Pattern, History, and Values.* West Chester, Pennsylvania: Schiffer Publishing Ltd., 1992.

_____. *Historic Flow Blue.* Atglen, Pennsylvania: Schiffer Publishing Ltd., 1994.

Worth, Veryl Marie, and Louise M. Loehr. *Willow Pattern China: Collector's Guide.* Rev. 4th ed. H. S. Worth Co., 1991 (distributed by Louise M. Loehr, Louise's Old Things, P.O. Box 208, Kutztown, PA 19530).

OTHER SCHIFFER TITLES

Willow Ware Leslie Bockol. Willow Ware, the blue transfer printed pattern that is possibly the most popular single pattern of ceramic dishes, is presented with makers, dates, marks and range of values. Hundreds of clear color photographs show the many styles and range of quality.

Size: 8 1/2" x 11"   475 color photos   160 pp.
Price Guide
ISBN: 0-88740-720-X   soft cover $29.95

Introducing Roseville Pottery Mark Bassett. Roseville pottery was made from 1890 to 1954. Here over 840 color photographs present numerous product lines, a discussion of experimental and trial glaze pieces, a glaze and shape identification guide, a timeline of Roseville products, and the company's factory marks and artist signatures. Values are provided with a bibliography and an index.

Size: 8 1/2" x 11"   848 color photographs   288 pp.
Price Guide/Index
ISBN: 0-7643-0921-8   soft cover $39.95

Adams Ceramics Staffordshire Potters and Pots, 1779-1998 David A. Furniss, J. Richard Wagner, and Judith Wagner. This is the most authentic and readable record of the prolific Adams ceramic wares from England, including earthenware, bone china, jasper, stoneware, basalt, and Parian made over a 200-year period. Over 1250 color photographs illustrate the comprehensive text.

Size: 9" x 12"   1250 photos   336 pp.
Price Guide/Index
ISBN: 0-7643-0847-5   hard cover $79.95

McCoy Pottery Jeffrey B. Snyder. Ceramics produced by the Nelson McCoy Pottery Company and its predecessor, the Nelson McCoy Sanitary Stoneware Company, are displayed in over 740 color photographs of utilitarian stonewares, cookie jars, beautiful artwares, and vases. A history of the companies, detailed discussion of McCoy manufacturing techniques, an examination of the manufacturer's marks, bibliography, appendix chronicling the many McCoy cookie jars, index, and values found in the captions make this a most useful guidebook.

Size: 8 1/2" x 11" over 740 color photos   208 pp.
Price Guide
ISBN: 0-7643-0804-1   hard cover $29.95

Flow Blue A Collector's Guide to Patterns, History, and Values *Revised 3rd Edition* Jeffrey B. Snyder. A new edition of a now-classic and thorough survey of highly prized ceramics with Flow Blue decoration. Color photos display changes in Flow Blue patterns of the Victorian Age. Includes photos of common and unusual manufacturers' marks, Flow Blue history, vessel forms and use, and dating techniques.

Size: 8 1/2" x 11"   over 500 color photos   160 pp.
Revised Price Guide
ISBN: 0-7643-0776-2   soft cover $29.95

Historic Flow Blue Jeffrey B. Snyder. This book puts Flow Blue in its historical context of the Victorian age. The British, American and European manufacturers who produced Flow Blue, the exhibitions that promoted it, the people who owned it and what moved them to buy it are explored. Over 500 color photographs present the variety of forms and patterns in these popular wares from the 1840s to the turn of the twentieth century.

Size: 8 1/2" x 11"   550 color photos   160 pp.
Price Guide
ISBN: 0-88740-640-8   soft cover $29.95

Fascinating Flow Blue Jeffrey B. Snyder. The focus is on Flow Blue ceramics products of English potteries, with beautiful examples from America and elsewhere included. There are lovely teapots, children's tea and dinner services, potpourri jars, pitchers, platters, and plates illustrated in color and identified.

Size: 8 1/2" x 11"   500 color photos   160 pp.
Value Guide
ISBN: 0-7643-0335-X   soft cover $29.95

Scottish Ceramics Henry E. Kelly. More than 630 striking color photographs showcase the multi-hued and widely exported dinnerware, vases, plaques, figurines, and other ceramics produced by the many Scottish potteries. Features brief histories of the potteries and wares produced, listings of forms and patterns, relevant readings, values, glossary, and index. An invaluable resource.

Size: 8 1/2" x 11"   631 color photos   208 pp.
Price Guide/Index
ISBN: 0-7643-0946-3   hard cover $59.95

Encyclopedia of Marks on American, English, and European Earthenware, Ironstone, and Stoneware: 1780-1980 Arnold A. & Dorothy E. Kowalsky. This essential new reference identifies thousands of marks from American, English and European potters. Marks are presented in alphabetical and chronological order by potters with historical facts. American and Canadian importers and the potters for whom they imported are identified. Ware types, printed patterns, registry dates, glossary and bibliography are included. Now identification of pottery has a single authoritative source.

Size: 8 1/2" x 11" 1719 printed manufacturers' marks 640 pp.
ISBN: 0-7643-0731-2   hard cover $69.95

Noritake Dinnerware: Identification Made Easy Robin Brewer. Noritake dinnerware now can be identified easily with the author's unique approach in finding a matching pattern or a similar shape that corresponds on his carefully compiled time line. Indexed by both name and number, the vast variety of Noritake dinnerware is displayed in over 1,200 color photos and described with price guide.

Size: 8 1/2" x 11"   1,258 color photos   192 pp.
Price Guide/Name and Number Indices
ISBN: 0-7643-0925-0   hard cover $39.95